Leadership: From Ordinary to Extraordinary: The Character of a Leader

Your Guide for Obtaining the 15 Qualities of an Extraordinary Leader

Stephanie A. Parson, Ph.D.
Foreword by Francis X. Taylor

Published by

CGI – International
A Crowned Grace Company
13506 Summerport Village Parkway, Suite 336
Windermere, FL 34786

CGI – International books and products are available through most bookstores. To contact CGI – call 866.544.6257 (toll free), fax to 321.251.5236 or visit our website at www.crownedgrace.com.

Substantial discounts on bulk quantities of CGI – International books are available to corporations, professional associations and other organizations. For details and discount information, contact the special sales department at CGI – International.

We at CGI – International strive to use the most environmentally sensitive paper stocks available to us. Our publications are printed on acid-free recycled stock whenever possible, and our paper always meets or exceeds minimum GPO and EPA requirements.

CGI – International also publishes its books in a variety of electronic formats. Some content which appears in print may not be available in electronic books.

Library of Congress Cataloging – in – Publication Data

Parson, Stephanie A., 1961 -
The charter of a leader: your guide to obtaining the 15 qualities of an extraordinary leader
ISBN 978-0-578-04870-3

1. Leadership. 2. Executive ability. 3. Management. 4. Self Improvement.

Foreword by Francis X. Taylor

I spent almost thirty five years serving our nation in ever increasing leadership roles from a counterintelligence analyst to the leader of two globally deployed federal investigative organizations. I am now a Vice President and Chief Security Officer for one of the world's best companies. Through all of those experiences, I have developed a very strong sense of what it takes to be a leader and where leaders fail.

I first met Dr (then Captain) Parson almost 15 years ago when she was a member of my command. I instantly marked her as a future leader in the Air Force. She had superb technical knowledge and could get Herculean work out of a small but integrated team. People respected what she said and what she did. I was very disappointed when she left the Air Force as I saw her career soaring; I now know that her horizons were far beyond those of the Air Force.

This book reflects how she has grown in her leadership journey and her ability to translate that journey into practical examples and simple questions to assess progress. In this book, Dr Parson has developed and presented a very straight forward and practical approach to understanding the principals of leadership allowing leaders and aspiring leaders to assess their own journey against those principals. As I read the book, I could not help but assess my own journey and where I would need to improve. The key here is that leadership is a continually - developing skill that the leader must work on constantly. Self-assessment, vision, humility and the ability to listen and receive feedback among all of the other traits are critical to sustaining yourself as an Extraordinary Leader.

I remain focused on this goal; with the help of Dr Parson's book will help me and you to do the same. I highly recommend this book to all those desiring to increase their abilities to lead in the 21st Century. From the individual contributor to the senior level executive – all will gain by going through this evolution.

Francis X. Taylor
VP & Chief Security Officer - The General Electric Company

Dedication

This could not have been completed without the encouragement and support of the following Extraordinary People:

my Advisory Board, the editorial team who took what was ordinary and made it extraordinary, graduates of our L:FO2E programs, my Mom & Dad and My Lord & Savior Jesus Christ

I would also like to thank YOU, the reader for taking the first step to becoming an extraordinary leader!

Thank you all!

Advance Praise

"Dr. Stephanie Parson has created a dynamic program that gets to the very heart of leadership. Quite often we talk about what leadership is and hope that we can somehow force ourselves into the 'perfect' mold envisioned for us. Dr. Parson's method strips the detritus from the theory in order to build a personal foundation from which everyone can develop as a leader. Her program is one of the finest examples of a whole-person approach; guiding the leader through the core of their spiritual, physical, mental and emotional selves to create a foundation on which leadership can be built."
Anthony S. Evangelista - President & CEO, Verihelion, Inc.

"In the sea of professional development books and self-help manuals, *The Character of a Leader* leadership manual easily sails to the forefront. Dr. Parson encourages individuals to consider a holistic view of themselves and recognize that they must achieve balance personally, professionally, physically, and spiritually in order to become extraordinary leaders. This book is for anyone who desires to move from ordinary to extraordinary and leave a legacy for generations to come."
Stacey L. Cobbs - Former CIO, Bowie State University

"By integrating her extensive leadership experience as a military officer, corporate executive and entrepreneur with her strong faith in God, Dr. Parson has produced an extraordinary book. You will love *The Character of a Leader* because you can immediately apply the principles in your personal, family, and business life."
Heather M. Gantt - Manager, Fortune 50 Entertainment Company

"I spent 34 years in the military, and was trusted with the command of five different organizations, including a fighter squadron and two fighter wings. Like most career military people, I felt like I understood all aspects of leadership. But there is a lot in this book that I found valuable and insightful, and (as painful as this is to admit), I learned a lot from it. I especially appreciate the thoughtful way Dr. Parson has integrated faith seamlessly into the discussion, as an inseparable part of a balanced life. I recommend this to anybody who is after life's rewards!"
Timothy Kinnan - Lt. General, USAF, Retired

"For those among us who were "born" leaders, Dr. Stephanie Parson has created a step-by-step process to unveil the leaders we were meant to be. From inspiration to education, you will be empowered to lead with conviction, purpose and strength. I strongly believe leaders in all stages will evolve into further effectiveness after completing this workbook."
Lexi Natello - CEO, DotCom Design Studio

"Dr. Stephanie Parson draws on her ever-growing body of knowledge and leadership skills to provide a holistic and comprehensive approach to leadership. In this book, she offers strategies, tools and techniques that will guide you on the path to your identifying your purpose and then further requests that you pinpoint that which keeps you from living our life based on your strengths. She then challenges you to become the champion of your own day!"
David M. Talon - Managing Partner, iGrowth Strategies

Introduction

The discipline of writing something down is the first step toward making it happen.
~ Lee Iacocca ~

Congratulations, you've just begun a personal journey of transforming your leadership style and capabilities. I am so proud of you as it takes courage to admit that there are still actions you can take to become an extraordinary leader. I am encouraged by your willingness to dig deep into your greatest strengths and greatest growth opportunities. Most importantly, I thank you for allowing me to share my 25+ years of experience in **ever becoming** an extraordinary leader!

I use the phrase "Ever becoming" because leadership is a choice one must make on a daily basis. How well you lead is dependent upon how well you desire to lead. Leading in the 21st Century is completely different from leading in the 19th and 20th centuries. The understanding of the differences between various generations, now categorized by using terms such as "Silent Generation", "Baby Boomers", "Generation X", "Generation Y", "Millennials" and Work–life balance continue to cause extraordinary leaders to learn, grow, improve and share their journey with others.

This leadership manual is built on the foundation of the premise that Leadership is a privilege, an honor and a choice. I believe that Extraordinary Leaders have three legs to balance: Leading Oneself before Leading Others, and Leading Others before they are given the responsibility of Leading Organizations. In other words, you must know how to lead yourself before given the privilege of leading others (teams, departments and/or families). Once you've proven yourself as a leader of people then and only then should you lead organizations.

The study method recommended for this journey revolves around four basic steps: observation, interpretation, correlation and application.

Observation – What does the text say? Interpretation – What does it mean to you? Correlation – In light of your experiences how does this relate to you, your team and/or your organization? Application – How should your leadership style be modified based on what you've learned? My recommendation is that you subscribe to CGI's monthly webcast and The New Face of Leadership™ magazine as you are going through this journey to enhance your leadership journey.

Some of you will rush through this Leadership Manual and others will take the time to really dig deep to ensure you have what you need to go to the extraordinary level of leadership. Still others will join us by attending our L:FO2E™ event, scheduling an L:FO2E™ event within your organization and/or by joining one our L:FO2E™ Inner Circle Groups to go through the entire process with other Extraordinary Leaders! Some of you will even purchase this Leadership Manual for your entire team and use it as a series of team development exercises! Whichever method you choose … enjoy the journey and Lead an Extraordinary Life … Today!

Dr. Stephanie A. Parson

P.S. Every month, coaches, leaders and authors provide their insight to various aspects of leadership in The New Face of Leadership™ magazine. To receive a complimentary copy, go to

CrownedGrace.com/tnfol_magazine

The Character of a Leader

Your Guide for Obtaining the 15 Qualities of an Extraordinary Leader

Your Core Essence
Extraordinary Leaders Know Their Purpose

1. Observation
2. Interpretation -- Why Were You Created?
3. Correlation
4. Application

Observation

Understanding your Core Essence, your reason for being, is the first step toward becoming an extraordinary leader; however, very few ever take the time to understand their reason for being, their reason for their existence. Is there any wonder that there are so many people trying to find themselves? Yet when we were asked as children what we wanted to become, most of us knew the answer or our parents told us things like, "You always were building airplanes/ trying to make movies/ telling stories / singing or _____."

Do you remember how you answered that question – "What do you want to be when you grow up?" Though your occupation is not your purpose – it can be an indicator of whether you stayed the course of who you were destined to become!

Did you stay the course?

Along the way, most of us were "talked out" of our purpose. What did you want to do when you grew up?
Are you in a field related to what you wanted to become?

The mother of a famous baseball player was asked when her son knew he wanted to become a baseball player. She quickly replied, "Before he was eight years old, he told us that he was going to be in the Major League. Right after high school, he was drafted into the Minor League and in 2008 he was touted as 'one of the most prolific home run hitters in baseball history."

Again, your vocation is not your purpose. However, if you know your purpose, the reason for your existence, then the education, positions and opportunities you take become more meaningful … driving you to complete what you were created to do.

Here's another example. In viewing the Special Features of a M. Night Shyamalan movie one learns that he was already making films as a teenager. He knew he wanted to be a storyteller/film maker. What is it that you always wanted to do?

How many people have you met along your life's journeys who are on their third career? Or who are now doing what they always wanted to do? Many of us come across more people who are in the first group. What stops us from living life on purpose? For many it is our primary organizational code or family code. For example your family code may be:

- Finish high school
- Get a job, join the military or go to college
- Get married
- Have children, buy a house and get a better job
- Get promoted or get a better job
- Make money
- Repeat
- Retire and receive the "gold watch"

What if, as children, we were taught to develop in our purpose? How would our lives be different? What if, as children, we were taught to concentrate more on our strengths than our weaknesses? What if, as children, we were allowed to explore the various elements of our strengths? How would our lives be different?

Now, if you're reading this, it probably means that you cannot go back and relive your childhood – well I hope not anyway! However, you can take actions to determine your purpose now. I believe that extraordinary leaders have an understanding that there is a greater power than themselves - God. It is through this understanding that leaders are able to identify boundaries for the actions they take. Extraordinary leaders understand that their lives have more of a meaning in HIS overall plan than their own. And it is through the accomplishment of this plan - this purpose - this mission that ultimate fulfillment is attained. This fulfillment is that which Abraham Maslow identified as self-actualization – the instinctual need of humans to make the most of our abilities and to strive to be the best we can – working toward fulfilling our potential (purpose), and attempting to become all that we are capable of becoming.

Why Were You Created?

Complete the following statements:

I was created to accomplish the following:

_____
_____
_____
_____

I exist to serve by

_____
_____
_____
_____

Kevin McCarthy (2008) recommends using the following format: I exist to serve by [gerund, object]. For example: I exist to serve by Inspiring Hope.

In order to fulfill this purpose:

- I must take the following steps:
  - a.
  - b.
  - c.
  - d.

- I must look for the following types of education:
  - a.
  - b.
  - c.
  - d.

- I must look for the following opportunities:
  - a.
  - b.
  - c.
  - d.

Correlation

Share your purpose statement with 3 people and ask each of them

a. if this statement rings true.

b. to describe 3 instances in which they saw you living out this purpose.

c. to identify 3 people whom you could help by living out your purpose.

Identify five of your current activities which relate to the accomplishment of your purpose:

1._____

2._____

3._____

4._____

5._____

Identify three of your current activities which do not relate to the accomplishment of your purpose. Write your action plan for putting a stop to these activities. Find an accountability partner to ensure you are stopping these activities.

These activities do NOT align with my purpose	These are the action steps I will take to cease these activities	This person has agreed to be my accountability partner to ensure I stop working off-purpose

Application

> *Great minds have purposes, others have wishes.*
> ~ Washington Irving, 1783-1859 ~

Purpose means doing what you <u>know</u> you were created to do. Each job you have should drive you closer and closer to what you do best? I have found that I shine most when I am sharing with others, making it happen for others and of course speaking in front of large crowds. When did I find this out? In junior high school when I participated in my first performance touring group. In high school when I was told by my ROTC instructor that I was a wonderful speaker and found that I had more fun being a band announcer for the E.E. Smith Golden Bulls than being a pom pom girl (Are they stilled called this? And yes, I was a pom pom girl!).

For me, seeing others soar because of what I did to assist them is the coolest feeling and best accomplishment ever! What do you do that causes your coolest feeling? Explore that and determine how closely it is tied to your purpose.

Take time to determine your purpose. From this point forward take the actions which drive you toward your ultimate purpose. Use a **No Fear Here** mindset when taking on new roles and responsibilities which are more closely aligned to your purpose. If you are a parent, allow your children to find and live out their purpose - their core essence.

Extraordinary leaders know why they are here and strive to live out that reason!

Your Additional Thoughts

_____

_____

_____

_____

_____

_____

_____

_____

_____

_____

_____

_____

_____

_____

24 x 7 x 365 Days a Year
Extraordinary Leaders Lead - PERIOD!

1. Observation
2. Interpretation -- Let Your Hair Down and Lead an
   Extraordinary Life
3. Correlation
4. Application

Observation

Since being a leader is a choice and a responsibility, only those who are ready and willing should begin the journey of becoming an extraordinary leader. Being a leader is a 24-hours a day, 7- days a week, 365 days a year journey – not for the faint at heart! Many times ordinary leaders will try to escape their responsibilities by "letting their hair down". Did you know extraordinary leaders can also "let their hair down" without causing embarrassment to their family, their company or themselves? Understanding that no matter where you are in the world you are an extraordinary leader. Now this does not mean that you cannot relax; however, it does mean that when you relax you must do it in such a way that you would not mind if the whole world were watching. Extraordinary leaders take the time out to relax alone and with their family, friends and co-workers.

Is there ever a time when you stop being a leader? _____ We've all heard stories of leaders who are great at work but when you speak with their family, you discover that they are the worst family leader. We've also heard the stories of senior executives who decide to "let their hair down" and then find their pictures in the local tabloid!

The secret to "letting your hair down" and not showing up in the tabloids is that you should always keep in mind that you represent your family, your shareholders, your team members, your community and yourself. Now this does not mean that you live in a state of paranoia or that you never leave your house; it simply means that you live life in an extraordinary manner at all times!

Let Your Hair Down & Live an Extraordinary Life!

a. What do you do when you let your hair down?

_____
_____
_____
_____
_____
_____

b. If a press photographer took a picture of you during this time, what would your relatives, team members and shareholders think? Would they be excited or pleased with what they see on the front page? Why or why not?

_____
_____
_____
_____
_____
_____

Correlation

a. If you answered yes to the above question, what can you share with others so that they can also understand that leadership never stops?

_____
_____
_____
_____
_____

b. If you answered no to the above question, how can you do the same activity without making the front page news?

_____

_____

_____

_____

Application

The way to gain a good reputation is to endeavor to be what you desire to appear
~Socrates, 470-399 B.C. ~

It is difficult to count the number of times when, throughout my years in leadership, I was asked "Aren't you part of such and such organization?"- by someone I did not know and had never seen before. One specific episode stands out in my mind, I was adding additional lines to my home office and five minutes into the install, the cable guy turned and asked, "You're part of the _____ leadership team, right?" In my own home, in my own environment and in casual clothes, I was recognized by this man as a leader. This has happened to me at the grocery store, while in a different state catching a connecting flight and in so many other places. People know who you are and are hoping that you are the real deal!

Again, this doesn't mean that you are so bound that you cannot relax; it simply means that you relax in a manner that won't embarrass your parents, your spouse, your children, your company or your team. "What happens in _____, stays in _____!" Have you ever heard this statement? Extraordinary leaders don't believe this at all!

Because leadership is a privilege not a right, is not always associated with your title, you have the responsibility to conduct yourself as an extraordinary leader all the time!

Your Additional Thoughts

_____

_____

_____

_____

_____

_____

_____

_____

_____

_____

_____

_____

_____

_____

_____

Are You Fit?
Extraordinary Leaders Take Care of Themselves

1. Observation

2. Interpretation -- How Fit Are You?

3. Correlation

4. Application

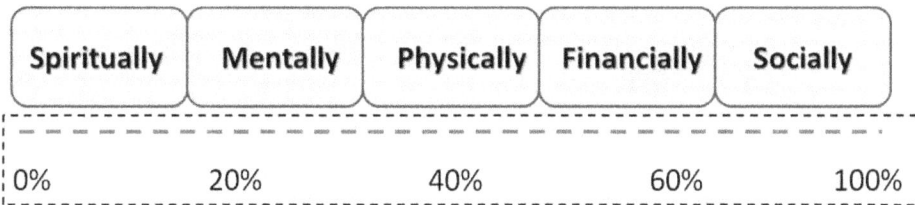

Observation

Talk to any great leader and they will tell you that they are active in having a balanced life -- balanced in the sense that every day they spend time ensuring wholeness by developing themselves spiritually, mentally, physically, financially and socially.

Each day you are presented with a gift of 1440 minutes. What do you do with this gift?

- o 14.4 minutes equals 1% of your day
- o 480 minutes are set aside for 8 hours of sleep
- o 480 minutes are set aside for 8 hours of work (Professional)
- o **YOU HAVE 480 minutes (8 hours) every day to build a balanced life (spiritual, mental, physical, financial and social)!**

Here are some tips on what you can do with that extra eight (8) hours:

- **Spiritually** - spending 15 minutes a day with your Creator is a little over 1% of your day.

    - Keep a journal and write down what your Creator says to you.
    - Ask HIM to describe what you should do that day.
    - Ask HIM to give you pointers on how you should resolve an issue at home, at the office or in the community.
    - Ask HIM for a BIG idea for that day.
    - Profess to yourself what HE says about you on a continual basis.
    - Imagine yourself living the life that HE created you to live: spiritually, mentally, physically, financially and socially. HE desires you to live in a life of abundance. What does that life look like?

- **Mentally** - Your drive to and from work is an excellent time to feed your mind and adds no additional time requirement to your day.

    - On your way to work listen to a CD or tape which allows you to feed your mind.
    - On your way home, spend quiet time allowing your mind to rest.
    - Do homework with your children. This will open you to developing new methods of learning and teaching others and will also allow you to spend more time with your family.
    - Stay consistent in implementing your learning work teams.
    - Don't forget to take care of your emotional side as well!

- **Physically** - take 2% of your day (30 minutes) and do an activity which will increase your heart rate (**Be sure to check with your doctor before starting any exercise program**).

- Make this a family activity in order to build family unity and instill in your children the importance of maintaining a healthy lifestyle.
- Make this an activity you do with your spouse. This will improve your spouse's health and help you to build a healthier relationship together!
- Take nutrients which enhance your own body's ability to produce what it needs to stay healthy.

- **Financially** - As a leader you must be financially sound

  - Many companies are now looking at an individual's credit report to determine if they should even hire the candidate.
    - Do you check your credit report on a quarterly basis?
      - Many credit reports have erroneous data in them. Unless you remove this information, your scores will be impacted by this erroneous data.
      - Checking your credit report also allows you to identify any one attempting to steal your identity before there is too much damage.

    - Are you taking actions to improve your BEACON score?
      - Making payments on time increases your score.
      - Not having too many credit cards increases your score.
      - Not allowing too many inquiries on your credit increases your score.

  - As a leader you should understand your department's budget and the budget process of your entire organization.

- Ask to participate in the development of departmental budget presentations.
- Understand how to read and discuss your company's annual report.
- Find creative ways to reduce cost or increase revenue within your organization.

○ As a leader at home look for ways to bring in residual income. Residual income translates to money while you sleep. In other words, even if you were unable to work again (layoffs, right sizing, companies closing, a new life direction) you would receive a pay check.
- Direct Marketing (Network Marketing)
- Real Estate Investments (Look at the portfolio of your favorite multi-millionaire and you will see real estate.)
- Teach your children the importance of supplemental – residual, money-while-you-sleep income
- Are you setting up an inheritance for your children's children?

- **Socially** – I must admit that area is my biggest challenge. However, I made a commitment to myself that I would begin to stretch myself and get out and have more fun! Being fit socially includes your family, spouse, children, love, sexual relations with your spouse and being active in your community. For me it meant being more flexible when I received a call at the last minute.
  ○ For those who are married or have significant others – have a date night once a week
  ○ For those with children – have a game night once a week
  ○ Join a committee within your community

How Fit Are You?

1. What are you currently doing with your gift of 1440 minutes each day?

_____
_____
_____
_____
_____

2. What percentage are you currently spending on developing your

  a. Spiritually? Describe what you currently do and with whom you do it:

_____
_____
_____
_____
_____

  b. Mentally/Emotionally? Describe what you currently do and with whom you do it:

_____
_____
_____
_____
_____

  c. Physically? Describe what you currently do and with whom you do it:

_____
_____
_____
_____
_____

d. Financially? Describe what you currently do and with whom you do it:

_____
_____
_____
_____
_____

e. Socially (Relationally)? Describe what you currently do and with whom you do it:

_____
_____
_____
_____
_____

3. Below define where you are now in each category by placing a number inside the circle outside of each category and then place a number in the square to define your desired state for each category.

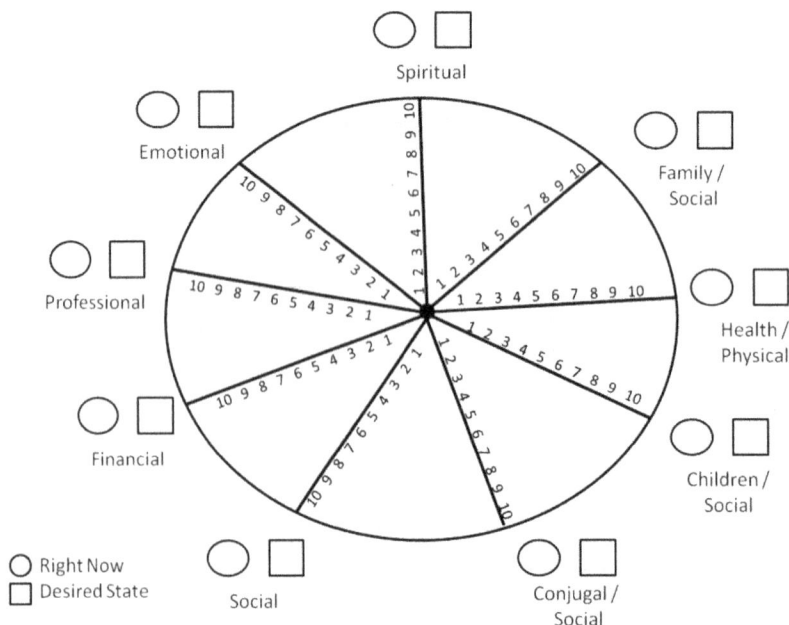

4. Complete the following equations by inserting the corresponding numbers from the previous graph and then subtracting your **Desired State** (number in the square) from your **Right Now** state (number in the circle):

Spiritual: ◯ - ▢ = _____   Family: ◯ - ▢ = _____

Health: ◯ - ▢ = _____   Children: ◯ - ▢ = _____

Conjugal: ◯ - ▢ = _____   Social: ◯ - ▢ = _____

Financial: ◯ - ▢ = _____   Professional: ◯ - ▢ = _____

Emotional: ◯ - ▢ = _____

5. In which area(s) are you over fit? (Numbers Greater Than One)
_____

6. In which area(s) are you un-fit? (Number Less Than One)
_____

7. In which area(s) are you fit? (Numbers Equal Zero)
_____

Correlation

In looking at your results from questions five and six:

1. Identify the steps you must take to become more

   a. Spiritually fit:
      1. _____

      2. _____

      3. _____

4. _____

b. Emotionally and Mentally fit:
1. _____

2. _____

3. _____

4. _____

c. Physically fit:
1. _____

2. _____

3. _____

4. _____

d. Financially fit:
1. _____

2. _____

3. _____

4. _____

e. Relationally (Socially, Family, Children, Conjugally) fit:
1. _____

2. _____

3. _____

4. _____

2. Select one item from each area which you will begin to implement today:
   a. Spiritual

   _____

   _____

   b. Mental

   _____

   _____

   c. Physical

   _____

   _____

   d. .Financial

   _____

   _____

   e. Relational

   _____

   _____

3. Select one item from each area which you will begin to implement in 30 days:
   a. Spiritual

   _____

   _____

   b. Mental

   _____

   _____

   c. Physical

   _____

   _____

d. Financial

_____

_____

e. Relational

_____

_____

4. Select one item from each area which you will begin to implement in 90 days:
    a. Spiritual

    _____

    _____

    b. Mental

    _____

    _____

    c. Physical

    _____

    _____

    d. .Financial

    _____

    _____

    e. Relational

    _____

    _____

5. Select one item from each area which you will begin to implement in 120 days:
    a. Spiritual

    _____

    _____

b. Mental

_____

_____

c. Physical

_____

_____

d. .Financial

_____

_____

e. Relational

_____

_____

6. In items 3 - 6, place a star by the items which you will do with your spouse.

7. In items 3-6, place a triangle by the items which you will do with your children.

8. In items 3-6, place a square by the items which you will do with your work team.

Application

You've got to get to the stage in life where going for it is more important than winning or losing.
– Arthur Ashe, 1943-1993 –

One of the biggest challenges you will have as an extraordinary leader is balance. Throughout my career, I have not met many executives who were able to "shut-down" or leave the office after eight hours. In fact, working twelve-hour days is more common as a result of a global economy and available technology. Even when the executive leaves the office he or she is still able to respond via email. Blackberrys, Blueberrys, Cell Phone, Laptops, Virtual Private Networks – all of these are great tools for the executive; however, they have also become a great burden. Your challenge is being able to say that when you leave the office, you're doing just that – leaving behind the office and the work you do there for the next day.

Of course there are times of emergencies when you must be tethered to the office when you leave; however, this MUST become the exception and not the rule. One C-level leader in a Fortune 100 company shared with her employer, employees and family that she will work as long as necessary to get a project done; however when she leaves the office for the day, she leaves work behind and becomes a wife and a mother.

What do you need to do to become fit – maintaining an appropriate work-life balance?

Extraordinary leaders understand that each day is a gift and using that gift requires a fitness level in your entire being: spiritually, mentally, physically, financially and socially!

Your Additional Thoughts

_____

_____

_____

_____

_____

_____

_____

_____

_____

_____

_____

_____

_____

_____

_____

_____

_____

Self Motivation
Extraordinary Leaders are Their Own Cheerleaders

1. Observation
2. Interpretation -- Two –, Four –, Six –, Eight, Who Do You
                         Appreciate?
3. Correlation
4. Application

Observation

Your biggest cheerleader and your most powerful critic is the person you see in the mirror every day. In fact, you believe your own voice more than any other voice you hear. Others may say things about you; but until you begin to think it, speak it and believe it; their words have no power over you. I want you to begin your day, each day from this point forward hearing words which will cause you to become the champion of your day.

Many of us allow our minds or the negative thoughts we have about ourselves, to determine how we perceive ourselves. How many times have you received a compliment and immediately responded with a negative attempt to discount the compliment?

As you are getting out of bed, the first thought which crosses your mind has the ability to define or control your day. Taking time each day to become your own cheerleader will not only set the tone for your day, but it will also set the tone for your family, your team and your organization.

Two –, Four –, Six –, Eight, Who Do You Appreciate?

Tonight, place a pen and this Leadership Manual next to your bed. When you wake up tomorrow, for the first five minutes, immediately begin to write down your thoughts. Write down exactly what you are thinking. Now, go back and circle those thoughts that you are having about yourself.

_____
_____

_____
_____

_____
_____

_____
_____

Next, get out of bed, go to your mirror and look at yourself from head to toe. Write down your thoughts, both positive and negative.

_____
_____

_____
_____

_____
_____

_____
_____

_____
_____

_____
_____

_____
_____

_____
_____

_____
_____

How many of your thoughts were positive? _____

How many of your thoughts were negative? _____

Correlation

a. Below, turn the above positive thoughts to statements of affirmation:

_____
_____
_____
_____
_____
_____
_____
_____
_____
_____

b. Below, turn the above negative thoughts to positive statements of affirmation:

_____

_____

_____

_____

_____

_____

_____

_____

_____

_____

_____

_____

_____

c. Now, go to someone in your Holy of Holies (the 5-7 people with whom you can be totally transparent) and ask that person to listen as you talk about yourself for 15 minutes. During that timeframe, this person is only allowed to say, "And what else?" At the conclusion of the 15 minutes ask your confidant if your self-talk created a more positive or more negative image about you. Record their response below:

_____

_____

_____

_____

_____

_____

_____

_____

_____

_____

d. At this time, write five concise sentences of positive affirmation about yourself:

_____
_____
_____
_____
_____
_____
_____
_____
_____
_____

e. For the next 90 days, before you leave for the day and as you are looking at yourself in the mirror, say these statements of affirmation to yourself - out loud.

f. If you are married, have children or have a beloved pet – write down five positive statements about each one. For the next 90 days speak these words into their lives each day before you (or they) leave the house.

g. For the next 90 days, make it a point to speak life into eight of your team members. Who are the seven in addition to you?

_____
_____

_____
_____

_____
_____

_____
_____

h. After 90 days, what changes have you seen:

in yourself?

_____
_____
_____
_____
_____
_____
_____

in your family?

_____
_____
_____
_____
_____
_____
_____

in your team?

_____
_____
_____
_____
_____
_____

i. At the end of 90 days, sit with a member of your family and a member of your team and ask them to describe themselves. What do they believe about themselves? Record their thoughts below:

_____
_____

_____

_____

_____

_____

j. Repeat this series of exercise at least three times a year.

k. Always remember that you are wonderfully made for a specific purpose!!!

Application

I was always looking outside myself for strength and confidence, but it comes from within. It is there all the time.
~ Anna Freud, 1895-1982 ~

I've discovered that the first step in coming out of a hard time begins with me reminding myself of who I am and encouraging myself. You may recall that an extraordinary leader named David could not come out of his cave until he encouraged himself. When I've gone through these hard times, friends have tried to encourage me through their words or deeds – that's what friends are for! However, as they were edifying, the voice in my own head was louder. So, yes, I do talk to myself ... out loud even! My words, spoken out loud, must echo what my Creator says about me. My words, spoken out loud, must prepare me for what may come. My words, spoken out loud must encourage, empower and enable.

Parents, you must know that your voice is the most important voice your children will hear for years after you've made the statement. It is the same for spouses. What are you speaking into the lives of the people you care about on a daily basis?

Your desire to be an extraordinary leader must be greater than your level of fear. Any fear which comes your way can easily be conquered if you will only profess what you know to be true! Extraordinary leaders edify themselves and those around them every day!

You are wonderfully made!

Anything which comes up today, you were already created to resolve with excellence!

You always persevere under trial with great success!

Your Additional Thoughts

_____

_____

_____

_____

_____

_____

_____

_____

_____

_____

_____

_____

_____

_____

Learn, Unlearn, Relearn
Extraordinary Leaders Know the Power of Change

1. Observation
2. Interpretation -- How Are You Staying Abreast of Change?
3. Correlation
4. Application

Observation

As an extraordinary leader, you must make a point to continuously develop yourself. What are you reading? What are you listening to in your car? It is important that you understand your personal trade or discipline, but you must also understand the industry of your organization. For example, if you are in the finance department in an engineering firm you must stay abreast of the changes in the finance discipline as well as what is going on within the engineering discipline. The more you know about both disciplines, the better positioned you are for higher levels of management and leadership.

The higher your organizational level, the more difficult it is to stay up to date on your personal discipline. You can do this by creating learning teams within your organization. Here's a great tip to develop yourself and your team: assign individuals members to "stay abreast" of a particular area within their discipline and have the team members train the group on a monthly or quarterly basis.

- For Example: If your team is responsible for sales and marketing you can identify a team member as the learning leader for
    - Sales & Marketing Technology
    - Sales & Marketing Processes
    - Sales & Marketing Legal/Governmental Mandates

- Sales & Marketing Customer Relations Modeling

- These learning teams will
  - Identify your group as the team with the most current knowledge of the industry
  - Prepare your team members to present to senior levels of management
  - Build confidence in your team members
  - Build cohesiveness within your team
  - Identify you as a great team leader

You should never allow the statement "We've always done it that way" to come out of your mouth. As a leader, you have to unlearn old thinking and allow new thinking to keep you abreast of your world. Always be open to change - as long as it does not go against your core essence or your core values.

How Are You Staying Abreast of Change?

1. Identify 5 methods you use to stay abreast of changes within your own discipline.
   a. _____
   b. _____
   c. _____
   d. _____
   e. _____

2. What types of learning teams do you need to create to stay abreast of your technical discipline?
   a. _____
   b. _____
   c. _____
   d. _____
   e. _____

3. Who should lead the learning teams you identified above?

   a. _____
   b. _____
   c. _____
   d. _____
   e. _____

4. What habit or belief system ("We've always done it that way") are you holding on to?

   a. _____
   b. _____
   c. _____

Correlation

1. For the next 90 days, listen to a tape or CD on an area in which you need to come up to speed (your technical discipline, finance, starting a business, real estate investment, etc.). Listen to one tape every day on your way to work.

   a. What did you learn during this 90-day journey?

      1. _____
      2. _____
      3. _____

   b. What can you implement immediately?

      1. _____
      2. _____

   c. What can you implement in 60 days?

      1. _____
      2. _____

2. Select one habit from **How Are You Staying Abreast of Change** which you need to unlearn. What steps do you need to take to unlearn this habit or behavior?

   a. _____

   b. _____

   c. _____

   d. _____

   e. _____

3. Over the next 60 days, implement the steps you identified to unlearn a habit or behavior. You may wish to make this a personal habit. For example, if you decide that "I need to stop eating the entire gallon of ice cream", one step you may want to take is to drink two glasses of water each time you want ice cream to quench the desire to snack.

4. Schedule your first learning team meeting in 30 days. Complete the following statement. Once it is completed, immediately share it with your team, mentor, leader & sponsor:

   "I, _____, will host our first learning team meeting on _____."

Application

The only thing we know about the future is that it will be different.
~ Peter F. Drucker, 1909-2005 ~

I began my career as a technologist. In fact, there was a time when I wrote code using machine language or worse, using punch cards. While teaching a class in programming languages, I asked my students if they knew what punch cards were. I received only blank stares. How successful would I be if I were still using punch cards to develop software?

Currently, I am going through a personal journey of identifying habits that I've been holding onto which lead to no avail. My grandfather will turn 97 this year; I wonder how many of his beliefs have changed because of the advancements made by mankind. What are you holding onto that is keeping you from moving forward? What if it is keeping your children from moving forward with their lives? Perhaps it is inhibiting your team or organization. Be honest – what habit is holding you back from your future?

As an extraordinary leader, you embrace change! You are a change agent!

As an extraordinary leader, you are able to adjust to change … as long as it doesn't go against your core essence!

Your Additional Thoughts

_____

_____

_____

_____

_____

_____

_____

_____

_____

_____

_____

_____

_____

_____

Get Up!
Extraordinary Leaders Use Adversity as a Propellant

1. Observation
2. Interpretation – Using Adversity to Propel You to Extraordinary
Levels of Leadership
3. Correlation
4. Application

Observation

In my own life's journey, I've discovered that we all go through some level of adversity; in fact, I believe you are either going through an adverse situation, coming out of an adverse situation or going into an adverse situation. It is part of the circle of life. As extraordinary leaders, our goals should be to come out of every adverse situation wiser, stronger, better, more compassionate, and with a stronger desire to help others learn from the lessons we learned while going through such adversity.

Adversity can come in the form of a job loss, business failure, foreclosure, divorce, loss of a family member, bankruptcy, betrayal, retirement, conflict at home or in the workplace, etc. It also comes in different levels of severity. Whatever it looks like, whatever it feels like - adversity comes. It can lead one to a total breakdown or a total victorious breakout. It can cause you to give up, cave in and quit.

OR it can cause you, the extraordinary leader, to propel to higher levels of leadership!

The Great Depression (1929- 1930s), a dramatic worldwide economic downturn was the largest and most important economic depression in world history. If we look at our history books, we discover how many people in different countries reacted to this timeframe of adversity. Some gave up and quit life, while others persevered; still others were able to propel to extraordinary levels of greatness. As individuals, while going through our own *great depression* we have to make the decision to give up and cave in or, persevere and learn from this time period in order to and use it as a spring board to our next level. We choose!

Through many of our Leadership: From Ordinary to Extraordinary™ (L:FO2E) workshops, we have found leaders who have not reached their extraordinary level because of a past trial, tribulation or adverse situation. They were holding on to an angry feeling, a moment of betrayal which prevented them from being 100% extraordinary. Many leaders did not even recognize that a past adverse situation was preventing them from moving forward. During one L:FO2E™ workshop, an attendee from the federal government had a major breakthrough. At the end of that day, the attendee immediately called home to confirm that the anger and frustration being held on to for over ten years had caused problems within the family and past employers.

Many people believe that adversity in one's personal life does not impact one's business life. Studies prove over and over that this is not true. This is one of the reasons many companies began to take on a *work-life* balance mentality. Later in this manual, we will talk about the different types/levels of conflict. For now, understand that the correlations between the two types of conflict, internal and interpersonal, have a direct impact on the workforce. Conflict is a form of adversity.

As shared earlier, adversity will come in your personal life and your business life. How you decide to handle the adversity will determine if it hinders you or propels you to higher levels of leadership.

Use Adversity to Propel You to Extraordinary Levels of Leadership

Below, describe the past 24 months in your life, specifically focusing on an area in which caused the highest level of adversity in your life.

The situation:

_____
_____
_____
_____
_____
_____
_____
_____
_____
_____
_____
_____

What role did you play in causing this adversity? You must be honest regarding your role in the situation.

_____
_____
_____
_____
_____
_____
_____
_____
_____
_____
_____
_____

Who was involved in causing the adversity?

_____
_____
_____
_____
_____
_____

_____
_____
_____

How did you (do you) feel while going through this adversity?

_____
_____
_____
_____
_____
_____
_____
_____
_____
_____

What about your life changed (is changing) because of this challenge?

_____
_____
_____
_____
_____
_____
_____
_____
_____
_____

What did you discover about yourself because of this challenge?

_____
_____
_____
_____
_____
_____

_____
_____
_____
_____
_____

Who stood by you during this time period?

_____   _____   _____
_____   _____   _____
_____   _____   _____

How will your life be different because of this challenging episode in your life?

_____
_____
_____
_____
_____
_____
_____
_____
_____
_____
_____

Correlation

According to Krovetz (1999), every person has the ability to overcome adversity when protective factors are present. This is known as the resiliency theory. The protective factors described by Krovetz include:

- social competence - the ability to establish and maintain positive relationships

- problem solving skills - planning that facilitates seeing oneself in control and resourcefulness in seeking help from others
- autonomy - a sense of one's own identity and an ability to act independently and exert some control over one's environment
- a sense of purpose and future - goals, educational aspirations, persistence, hopefulness and a sense of a bright future
- positive expectations - high, clearly articulated expectations
- participation - meaningful involvement and responsibility

As an extraordinary leader, you must always know that you can and will overcome adversity. The wise person may fall seven times, but their wisdom is only discovered during their process of getting up each time. What are you doing to ensure that your protective factors are always present?

What have you done to maintain the positive relationships of those who assisted you during your time of adversity? If you have not maintained the relationships, what could you do to re-establish and improve these relationships?

1. _____
2. _____
3. _____
4. _____
5. _____

When asked what kept the leaders from being 100% extraordinary, one response was that they were still holding onto a portion or all of the anger they had towards the person, group of people or employer who caused the situation to occur.

Who do you need to forgive for their part in this adversity? Forgiveness releases you to the possibilities which await you. It has little to do with the person you are forgiving. Forgiveness allows you to release the *control* that person, memory or event has over you. How do you know when that entity has control over you? If you still get angry, frustrated or stuck because of a memory – it has control over you. We have a wonderful forgiveness exercise located on our website, www.crownedgrace.com/forgiveness, through which many people have received the release they needed to move forward. Keep in mind that you may have to go through the exercise many times before you are able to truly forgive and move forward. Who do you need to forgive to move towards your extraordinary greatness?

_____   _____   _____

_____   _____   _____

If you were to share your story with three people who may be going through something similar, what would you share and how would you encourage them to persevere?

_____
_____
_____
_____
_____
_____
_____

Application

Initially, I was not going to include this chapter in this leadership manual; however, after receiving feedback from many of the leaders who read this manual I decided to add a chapter on adversity. Their feedback is that one area which is part of the journey of an extraordinary leader is learning how to handle a major setback and thrive afterward.

One of my major life trials was the loss of a job which had a very lucrative compensation package. The loss of the job was not the big issue, although I did miss the compensation package; the circumstances surrounding the loss and the person behind the loss was the bigger issue. What do you do when a person does everything in their power to destroy you and your reputation? What do you do when the event has an impact on every aspect of your life?

For me, the answer was surrounding myself with strong people who I respected who had been through a similar experience. It also meant going back to my core essence and remembering that my purpose was and is not related to a position. It meant picking myself up (with the assistance of family and friends) and moving forward...and moving forward...and moving forward.

Is it always easy? No. Were there moments of anger? Yes. Were there thoughts of caving in and quitting? Yes. However – quitting is not an option! Living in a state of anger is not an option! Hearing "well done" at the completion of my purpose is the only option.

An extraordinary leader may fall seven times ... but each time the leader will get up!

Your Additional Thoughts

_____

_____

_____

_____

_____

_____

_____

_____

_____

_____

_____

_____

_____

_____

_____

Outer Court, Inner Court, Holy of Holies
Extraordinary Leaders Surround Themselves with Great People

1. Observation
2. Interpretation -- Surround Yourself With Great People
3. Correlation
4. Application

Observation

A team is a group of individuals working together toward a common goal. It can be self-directed or leader-directed, temporary or permanent. It can consist of internal and external members. Extraordinary leaders have three types of teams:

- **Outer court** - consists of the masses: peers, co-workers, employees, acquaintances
- **Inner court** - consists of other leaders, family members, mentors and friends
- **Holy of Holies**
    - Within an organization
        - Your leader
        - Your direct reports
        - Your key mentor
        - Your sponsor
    - Within your family
        - Your Creator
        - Your spouse
        - Your best friend
        - Depending on their age, this can also include your children

- Within your **Holy of Holies**
  - You must have people with whom you can be transparent.
  - You must have people who will allow you to be transparent with them.
  - You must have people who will hold you accountable in your actions and deeds.
  - You must have people who will assist you in developing and implementing your vision and purpose.
  - You must have people you trust and respect.
  - These are the people with whom you will share a strategic thought and ask them to tear it apart and help you put together a better thought.
  - These are the people with whom you can be vulnerable enough to share your concerns, fears and doubts.
  - These people are your biggest cheerleaders.

- Within your **Inner Court** you find
  - Mentors
  - Peers
    - Within your department
    - Within your organization
    - Within key associations
  - Relatives
  - People who work for your direct reports
    - They add the hands and feet to implement the vision
  - Key vendors / partners
    - They provide the resources required to implement your vision
  - Your **Inner Court** allows you to
    - Put action to your vision
    - Create strategic relationships within your organization, association and/or community

- Within your **Outer Court** you find:
    - The remaining portion of your department
    - The community at large

- Types of information you share with
    - **Holy of Holies**
        - Your entire plan for your department (your key mentor, your leader and/or your direct reports)
        - Your career aspirations (your spouse, your sponsor, your key mentor)
        - Your life's aspiration (your spouse, your sponsor)

    - **Inner Court**
        - The strategic direction for your department
        - Expectations of your department
        - Feedback on the entire department
        - Requirements from others to be successful in the strategic direction of your department

    - **Outer Court**
        - The strategic plan (with associated projects) for your department
        - Department objectives and goals

- Types of information you receive from
    - **Holy of Holies**
        - Honest feedback on you, your life, your actions, your deeds
        - Constructive criticism on all areas of your life

    - **Inner Court**
        - Honest feedback on your visions and plans
        - Constructive feedback on the health of your organization
        - What is not working well within the organization/department/team/family

- Status of the organizational health

  o **Outer Court**
    - Feedback on organizational direction
    - Comments/concerns of the team leaders
    - Feedback on what is working well throughout the organization
    - Feedback on what is not working well throughout the organization

Surround Yourself With Great People

1. Identify 3-5 people within your Holy of Holies:

   1. _____
   2. _____
   3. _____
   4. _____
   5. _____

   2. Do they know that they are within your Holy of Holies?

   _____

   a. If yes, what are your expectations of them? What are their expectations of you?

   _____
   _____
   _____
   _____
   _____
   _____

   b. If no, what steps do you need to take to bring them into your Holy of Holies?

   _____

_____
_____
_____
_____
_____

    c. Why are they within your Holy of Holies?

_____
_____
_____
_____
_____
_____

    d. In what manner do you wish your Holy of Holies to hold you accountable?

        1. _____
        2. _____
        3. _____

3. What desires, challenges, opportunities and/or strategies do you need to share with them to help them assist you in meeting your personal objectives?

        1. _____
           _____
        2. _____
           _____
        3. _____
           _____

4. What desires, challenges, opportunities and/or strategies do you need to share with them to assist you in meeting your career objectives?

        1. _____
           _____

2. _____
    _____
3. _____
    _____

5. Repeat the same activities for your Inner Court and selected members of your Outer Court.

Correlation

1. Over the next 10 days, set an appointment with your **Holy of Holies** to discuss this concept. Discuss and develop your expectations for this relationship. Define a process which you will use with them to ensure you are held accountable by them.

2. Over the next 10 days, meet with your organizational **Holy of Holies** and discuss the strategic direction for your department. Ask them to identify any "red flags" which will prevent the team from meeting its strategic goals.

3. Develop a plan for your organizational **Holy of Holies** to meet with your **Inner Court** to develop the objectives and projects required to be successful with the vision for the organization.

4. After you have completed the activities for your Holy of Holies, complete the same exercise for both your **Inner Court** and your **Outer Court**.

Application

Individual commitment to a group effort -- that is what makes a team work, a company work, a society work, a civilization work.
~ Vince Lombardi, 1913-1970 ~

If you talk to the people within my Holy of Holies, they will tell you that I am a cautious person who is very slow to allow people into that sacred level of friendship. What happens when you are betrayed by someone within this group? This is perhaps one of the most painful journey's to go through. A couple of years ago, for the first time in my life, I took someone into my Holy of Holies and was betrayed. This person took what was personal to me, added their own 'spin' on my life and caused a series of negative activities. My level of trust in people went down quickly. In interviewing other leaders, I've found that these types of betrayals can come from a spouse, a family member, a co-worker, a boss or even a company.

How you handle this type of betrayal determines how you will handle all levels of relationships. To gain the most from this experience, I had to forgive and move forward, forgiving my betrayer but not forgetting the lessons learned by going through this journey. If I had chosen to hang onto the anger, the only people impacted by this would be me, others in my Holy of Holies and people with whom I would have relationships in the future. I wish I could tell you that the forgiveness occurred over night – it didn't. However it no longer impacts how I view new relationships.

I am a big believer in forgiving but without forgetting the lessons I learned through the process. Within my Holy of Holies, I need to be completely transparent in order to grow. What betrayal is holding you back from being transparent with your Holy of Holies, holding you back from becoming an extraordinary leader?

Outer Court: peers, co-workers, organizational leaders, employees & acquaintances
Inner Court: children, leaders, family, mentor, team leaders & friends
Holy of Holies: spouse, family, friends, direct reports

Extraordinary Leaders surround themselves with extraordinary people!

Your Additional Thoughts

_____

_____

_____

_____

_____

_____

_____

_____

_____

_____

_____

_____

_____

_____

_____

Influence
Extraordinary Leaders Influence More Than Manage

1. Observation
2. Interpretation -- Do You Influence or Do You Manage?
3. Correlation
4. Application

Observation

Today's organizational culture is a mixture of Baby Boomers, Generation X, Generation Y and Millennials. Retirees are returning to the workforce and diverse cultures with diverse belief systems are represented in the workplace. What the various groups desire from a leader (and an organization) has changed drastically over the last decade.

In yesterday's workforce, the desire of an employee was to obtain the *gold watch*. Working 15 hours a day was the expected norm from an employer and from the employee. Leaders used a style which was more transactional or command-and-control. Yesterday's employer focused on providing a *job* for their employees until retirement.

Today's employee focuses on *work-life balance*, being valued by the employer, advancement within the organization, benefits and perks.

Today's extraordinary leader must develop the ability to cause action to occur without 'bossing' people around. Many have heard children say, *you're not the boss of me!*; well that mindset now carries on to adulthood, where the people we manage expect to be treated as equal members of a team, each *playing* a separate role.

Extraordinary leaders are able to get people to do things that they do not fully understand or buy into - however since their leader asked them to do it, they do it with 100% of their effort. The people trust the leader and the leader's vision. We have all seen great examples (John F. Kennedy, Nelson Mandela and Gandhi) and we have seen bad examples in people and companies (Osama Bin Laden, Hitler, Jim Jones and Bernard Mattoff); both groups were able to influence people into action.

You are able to influence people into action by

- Gaining their trust by *walking the talk*
- Past performance of delivering on what's important
- Keeping the people's passion at the forefront of your thoughts, actions and deeds
- Being a person who can motivate through speaking (side note: if you are not comfortable in speaking in front of large crowds, join your local Toastmasters Club to obtain experience)
- *Fighting* on behalf of your people
- Being in a position of authority
- Being a person with a purpose (being on-purpose)

Do you influence or do you manage?

1. Ask 5 people you trust (a mixture of your Holy of Holies, Inner Court and Outer Court):

   1. If others trust you (write down their response)
      1. _____
      2. _____
      3. _____
      4. _____
      5. _____

   2. If you are seen as one who *walks the talk*

1. _____

2. _____

3. _____

4. _____

5. _____

3. If you are seen as one who delivers

    1. _____

    2. _____

    3. _____

    4. _____

    5. _____

4. If you are seen as a command and control type leader or a participatory type leader

    1. _____

    2. _____

    3. _____

    4. _____

    5. _____

2. Record yourself in delivering a 30 - 60 minute presentation

3. Have an independent person/organization critique your presentation skills by answering the following questions about your performance:

   1. When you speak do you speak with purpose?
   2. Do you speak with confidence?
   3. Do you speak with authority?
   4. Do you excessively use 'verbal' pauses ('umm', 'you know', 'like', 'and', etc.)?
   5. Are you motivating or de-motivating?
   6. Are you clear and concise?
   7. Write their comments below:

   _____
   _____
   _____
   _____
   _____
   _____
   _____

Correlation

Based on the comments you received above, select 3 areas in which you would like to see improvements and describe the improvement you would like to see.

1. _____
   _____
   _____
   _____
   _____
   _____

2. _____
_____
_____
_____
_____
_____

3. _____
_____
_____
_____
_____
_____

Select one of the three and develop a 60 day action plan. After 60 days, ask the same 5 people for their comments/thoughts. Once you have achieved the expected results, repeat this process until you have achieved improvement in all three areas.

_____
_____
_____
_____
_____
_____
_____
_____

Application

When ideas fail, words come in very handy
~ Johann Wolfgang von Goethe, 1749-1832 ~

The one category of people who understand the power of influence is the entrepreneur, especially those who are just starting a business with little or no start-up capital. Initially, they usually influence people to action simply based on their vision. After that, they are able to pull this same group of people into a long-term relationship – sometimes as an investor. I've had the opportunity to speak to over a thousand of entrepreneurs and it is interesting to watch how they are able to get the job done using other people's time, energy, expertise and/or money. What is it about successful entrepreneurs that enables them to influence people into action? Entrepreneurs are able to get people to act without any type of compensation; other than a promise, a hope and a dream.

Charismatic leaders also understand the power of influence. Many of us have been moved into action just by hearing someone speak; something they said and the passion behind what they said caused us to act - sometimes immediately!

Being able to influence is putting a voice to your passion, vision, energy, mission, integrity and purpose.

Extraordinary leaders get people to do something that they don't fully understand or buy into … but because of you, the extraordinary leader, they do it anyway!

Extraordinary leaders influence more than they manage!

Your Additional Thoughts

_____

_____

_____

_____

_____

_____

_____

_____

_____

_____

_____

_____

_____

_____

_____

_____

Don't Sweat the Small Stuff

Extraordinary Leaders Strategically Choose Their Battles

1. Observation
2. Interpretation - Know Your Own Buttons
3. Correlation
4. Application

Observation

- Have you ever found yourself
    - Continuously backing down on important issues?
    - Allowing unresolved situations to hurt important relationships?
    - Lashing out when dealing with difficult people?
    - Allowing people to continuously push your button?
    - Allowing conflict within your team to last beyond the initial disagreement?

If you answered yes to any of the questions above, then welcome to a great opportunity to improve your own leadership capabilities. Managing, resolving and leading through conflict is a key character trait of an extraordinary leader. In today's environment conflict can be described as

- Competitive or opposing action of incompatibles
- An antagonistic state or action
- Struggles resulting from incompatible needs, drives, wishes or demands
- A hostile encounter
- A foundation for creative solutions
- When competing responses are considered for a single event
- Both positive and negative for an environment

For every situation which comes your way, you have an opportunity to react with respect, with anger or not at all. Conflict is a situation in which you choose how you will react! Remember the television shows where the parent would count to ten before responding to a misbehaving child? Well it's in that 10 second count that allowed them to respond to the situation.

When was the last time you waited 10 seconds before responding to an issue? 5 seconds? 2 seconds? Pausing for 10 seconds allows you to reasonably respond to any issue that may come your way! Ten seconds allows you to ask yourself who should solve this problem – you or your team – and whether or not you should even be involved.

Extraordinary leaders understand that they should not fight every battle which comes their way. Remember, some battles are training grounds for your growth and some battles are training grounds for your team's growth.

Extraordinary leaders know there are people who do not think that they deserve what they have obtained. As an extraordinary leader, you must understand that these people – for whatever reason - believe they should have what you have. Most do not understand what you've gone through to obtain your level of success. Others may try with all their power to destroy your name and your reputation.

Many difficult situations will happen around you and to you; how you handle these situations determines your level of success.

Conflict has two faces; it can be either positive or negative. An extraordinary leader must recognize the power of both. Conflict can be:

Positive Because It Can Provide an Environment of	Negative Because It Can Provide an Environment of
• Increased Motivation • Enhanced problem/solution identification	• Decreased Productivity • Erosion of trust

- Group cohesiveness

- Reality adjustment

- Increased knowledge/skill
- Contribution to goal attainment
- Incentive for growth

- Coalition formation with polarized positions
- Secrecy and reduced information flow
- Morale problems
- Consumption of mass amounts of time
- Decision making paralysis

Types of Conflict Include:

In her book, How to Manage Conflict, Pickering (2000) shares the following:

1. **Internal Conflict** – disturbance which rages within an individual and reflects the gap between what they say they want and what they do about it. It can hamper and/or immobilize. Learn to recognize these levels within yourself, your family and your team members:

    1. Level 1: Headaches, backaches and tension

    2. Level 2: Burnout

    3. Level 3: Suicidal thoughts

2. **Interpersonal Conflict** – conflict between people or groups of people. This type of conflict, if unresolved will hamper and/immobilize.

    1. This type of conflict is often due to unfulfilled needs (being valued, not being in control, possessing low self-esteem, etc.). When needs are not met, people may retaliate, dominate, isolate themselves and/or passively cooperate (possessing a "don't care" attitude)

2. It can be: substantive conflict, personalized conflict or even communication problems

3. Three stages of interpersonal conflict include
    1. Everyday concerns and disputes
    2. More significant challenges
    3. Overt battles

Intervention Strategies Include

- Negotiation
- Mediation
- Arbitration
- Collaborating
- Compromise

Know Your Own Buttons!

Do you find yourself defending every action you take?

Yes _____ No _____

If yes, why:

_____
_____
_____
_____
_____

If no, why not:

_____
_____
_____
_____
_____

How should you handle conflict when it arises? First, you should ask for wisdom – it only takes 10 seconds! If we ask for help, we will receive the help we need to resolve any situation. Extraordinary leaders open themselves to receive assistance from others. Second, determine how much you (or the group) know about the issue to be resolved.

Next, determine if you have the authority to make the decision. How much leverage can you bring to resolve the conflict? Are you the final decision maker or is there another person? How much power does the other party have over you or the final decision? Should the decision be made at your level or at a higher or lower level?

You develop extraordinary leaders by allowing your team members to resolve conflict at their level.

Determine the following: do you *have* to win or does the other party *have* to win? Is compromise acceptable or is losing acceptable? Remember, in some cases, allowing the other party to *win* allows you a more strategic win in the future.

Key points for selecting an approach

- Lead from strength
- Set the climate
- Assess the situation
- Clarify the issues
- Encourage equal participation
- Encourage active listening
- Look for commonalities
- Evaluate alternative approaches
- Step back, differentiate fact from opinions and focus on the problem, not the people
- Allow time to evaluate and make decisions
- Solve the problem

Correlation

1. List 7 people in your organization, team or community with whom you are in conflict:

Name	Overview of Conflict (Substantive, Personal, Communication Problems?)	Strategy for Resolving Conflict (Negotiation, Mediation, Arbitration, Collaborating, Compromise)	Who is the Right Person to Resolve?	Results/Follow-up Actions Required

Identify four (4) groups with whom your team has conflict and which you have the authority and power to resolve. As a team, develop the appropriate resolution strategy.

1._____

_____

_____

_____

_____

_____

_____

_____

2._____

_____

_____

_____

_____

_____

_____

_____

3._____

_____

_____

_____

_____

_____

_____

_____

4._____

_____

_____

_____

_____

_____

_____

_____

For the next five days, document at least two times where you found yourself defending a decision or an idea or a subordinate.

Situation 1: What was the decision/idea/person you were defending?

_____

_____

What action did you take?

_____

_____

Who were the people in the room? What was their affiliation with the situation?

_____

_____

After two days, if you had to do it again, what would you change about the situation?

_____ _____

_____

_____

_____

Situation 2: What was the decision/person you were defending?

_____

_____

What action did you take?

_____

_____

_____

_____

_____

Who were the people in the room? What was their affiliation with the situation?

_____

_____

_____

After two days, if you had to do it again, what would you change about the situation?

_____

_____

_____

_____

Self Reflection: in those times where you've "blown it", what could you have done to react differently? Complete the following: I've noticed that whenever _____

is involved with a decision, I tend to over react or act out of anger.

Therefore, I will take the following five steps to ensure I am better able to handle this person/situation in the future:

1. _____

_____

_____

_____

2. _____

_____

_____

_____

_____

3. _____

_____

_____

_____

4. _____

_____

_____

_____

5. _____

_____

_____

_____

Application

> *Even a mistake may turn out to be the one thing necessary to a worthwhile achievement.*
> ~ Henry Ford, 1863-1947 ~

In my own development journey, I must admit that the method which I often handled conflict was to win by almost any means necessary. I would not back down. The earliest episode I can recall is when I was a pre-teen living in Germany, weighing 80 pounds, responding to conflict by challenging a teenage boy who weighed at least 130 pounds to a fight. I couldn't back down! Looking back, I wonder, "What was I thinking?" As I grew older, I handled conflict in a similar manner, while I didn't actually fight for a resolution, I maintained the position of a fighter.

During my military period, I began to notice that people often "push buttons" on purpose, to get a reaction. In corporate America, I had a co-worker who enjoyed doing this to peers. To this day, I believe that doing this is a waste of energy. And yet, recognizing what this behavior caused me to do allowed me to determine what my own buttons were (are) and then develop my own strategies to only show the reaction I wanted to show. Does this make sense?

I will never purposely push someone to conflict or anger – that is not the action of an extraordinary leader. However, I am smart enough to know that there are people who do. What I've discovered is that the person who pushes buttons gets confused and frustrated when they are no longer able to get a reaction out of me. What are your buttons?

_____

Another critical area of self-discovery is how I handle stress. By design, I am a strategically visionary person. Under stress these traits are multiplied by tens of thousands.

Under normal circumstances, I will the journey by identifying major milestones which should occur throughout the journey. When under stress there are two points on the journey, we are here today and this is where we need to be tomorrow – go and do! For some of my team members, there was no problem with this approach; however, for some who needed more milestones, this approach was very frustrating.

Since I know this part of me, it is up to me to know when my own buttons are being pushed (stress indicators) and ensure that I am able to deliver the messages in a manner in which all can understand, in a way which will help everyone move forward. How do you behave when you are under stress?

_____

_____

_____

Extraordinary leaders know which battles to fight, which battles to pass on to others and which battles to walk away from. What battles are you fighting and why?

Your Additional Thoughts

Don't Get Too Big For Your Britches

Extraordinary Leaders Get Involved

1. Observation
2. Interpretation - Get Muddy While You Teach Your Eaglets to Fly
3. Correlation
4. Application

Observation

"Because I'm the boss and you have to do what I say!"

Believe it or not, there are people who still manage others from this perspective. Well, the days of leaders sitting in their ivory tower, watching over the employees from afar are long gone. Today's leader looks for ways to involve themselves in the inner workings of their area of responsibility.

Look at the eagle and take on some of her characteristics. For example, eagles know when to soar on the winds and when to dive in deep. As an extraordinary leader, you will need to know when to dive into the details (tactical) and when to rise to the higher heights (strategic).

Today's workforce wants you to know the joy and the pain of the workday and when necessary, to get involved. At a bare minimum, they want you to provide air cover – looking out on the horizon to ensure they are going in the right direction and to providing protection as needed. One intriguing characteristic of the eagle is that she never stays on the ground too long.

Leaders who stay in the tactical arena too long become known as micromanagers.

Today you're expected to lead and to develop leaders. Eagles develop their eaglets by providing them opportunities to learn. For example, when it's time for the eaglet to fly, the eagle makes the nest a little uncomfortable. You can do this with your team members by providing them with stretch assignments. As they begin to acquire the needed skills, stretch them even further.

As you are watching the eagle, you'll see that she then nudges the eaglet out of the nest, allowing the eaglet to exercise its wings. No fear here! If the eaglet doesn't effectively use its wings to fly, the eagle swoops down and saves the eaglet. She continues to present the eaglet the same opportunity until the eaglet "gets it" and flies.

You can do this with your team by providing your team members with progressively growing responsibilities. Allow them to stretch their wings by developing solutions in their own manner while you provide the boundaries. Watch from a distance, be available when needed and only swoop in when it is absolutely necessary. Your eaglet will soon be prepared to handle much larger responsibilities.

Get Muddy While You Teach Your Eaglets to Fly

a. Describe times in your own leadership journey when you found yourself being micromanaged. What was going on at the time within the organization? Within the team? How did you feel at the time?

_____
_____
_____
_____
_____
_____

b. What six actions could you have done to cause your leader to have more confidence in you and your ability to accomplish the task?

_____

_____

_____

_____

_____

_____

c. Describe a time where you found yourself micromanaging a team member. What was going on that caused you to micromanage?

_____

_____

_____

_____

_____

_____

d. What six actions could your team member have done to obtain your confidence on the task?

_____

_____

_____

_____

_____

_____

e. What six actions could you have taken to let your team know that you had confidence in them to complete the task?

_____
_____

_____
_____

_____
_____

Correlation

The sooner you teach your eaglets to fly, the higher you are allowed to fly. During this series of actions, you will further develop your own skill sets, allowing your teams may soar with confidence!

a. Of the items you identified in 2b, 2d and 2e, which four actions will you begin to take over the next 60 days?

_____
_____

_____
_____

b. Meet with someone within your leadership (Inner Court or Holy of Holies) and share the four areas you have committed to working on and ask them to give you instant feedback when you slip back into old behavior. Who is the person you selected as your accountability partner? _____ Commit to contacting them within 24 hours.

c. Of the items remaining in 2b, 2d and 2e, choose four items you can commit to modifying within an additional 90 days. Which items did you select?

_____

_____

_____

_____

d. Repeat step 3b.

e. Every 30 days, check in with your accountability partner to find out how you are doing.

f. What changes are you seeing in your team members?

30 days

_____

_____

_____

_____

60 days

_____

_____

_____

_____

90 days

_____
_____

_____
_____

120 days

_____
_____

_____
_____

Application

There is no such thing as a self made man. You will reach your goals only with the help of others.
~George Shinn~

While in the United States Air Force, I had the opportunity to be stationed at a remote location in Alaska, a place known for its King Salmon. Every year when the salmon were spawning, we would have a senior officer visit for a base tour. On one specific occasion, we had to ensure that the base was spotless. This included seeing to it that all trash was picked up. Now, this was right after the snow melted and the area assigned to my flight was muddy – almost swamp like. No matter what type of spin we put on this activity, for my troops, it meant getting muddy and dirty.

My options were as follows – direct (order) my flight to get muddy while I drove around and pointed out the garbage OR put on my mucklucks and get in the mud alongside my flight. I chose the latter – not expecting anything other than letting my team know that I was there with them and that I wasn't too big for my britches.

The comments I received from my team have remain with me to this day. For example, one of my 15 year Master Sergeants, Bear, shared that I was the best officer he had served under. To this day, I still tear up thinking about these comments. The simple act of letting your teams know that trust them to fly solo but are there for them when the going gets tough (or muddy) will go miles!

Extraordinary leaders know when to pitch in and when to allow their team members to fly!

Become the eagle!

Your Additional Thoughts

_____

_____

_____

_____

_____

_____

_____

_____

_____

_____

_____

_____

_____

Can You Be Touched?
Extraordinary Leaders Understand the Power of the Soft Side of Leadership

1. Observation
2. Interpretation - Share Your Personal Best & Your Personal Worst
3. Correlation
4. Application

Observation

Today extraordinary leaders have the wonderful opportunity to be so much more than yesterday's leaders. Yesterday's leader often hid behind their titles, their ranks or their office doors – never getting to know the people on their teams and never sharing their lives with their teams. Sometimes, yesterday's leader could not distinguish between the office, home or community; because they were trying to be *"the leader"* they forgot to be *"a leader"*.

An extraordinary leader understands how to engage others on a personal level. This personal level can include sharing success stories about their children, accomplishments of a community team or something as simple as achieving a life goal. In our LFO2E™ programs we encourage a discussion called *"What's So Cool About Being Me!"* During this session we ask the participants to share three things with others which have nothing to do with their work life or their education. It is at this level of openness and engagement that people build relationships.

People spend over 30% of their lives in the workplace, so it is not uncommon for *life matters* to come into the workplace, matters that are both positive (such as births, weddings, anniversary, etc.) and the negative (such as death, divorce, illness, and/or loss of a job). Be bold enough to share your positive and your negative life experiences with others in the workplace. Now this does not mean that you are coming to work with "all your business in the streets". It simply means that you share more of you with those who matter. You will see a dramatic difference in how coworkers interact with you and will often find that they become more open with you, simply because you took the time to share your life with them.

This openness provides an avenue for the extraordinary leader to build a heart connection with their spouses, their children, their families, their teams and within their work environment. The extraordinary leader understands that this is the basis of the power of influence. Once you're able to make a heart connection, your team will know that you are a *"real"* person because you share similar values, goals, experiences, trials and accomplishments. Once your team can see that you are like them, they will be able to trust you to make decisions which will benefit everyone.

Share Your Personal Best & Your Personal Worst

Identify five personal best stories which you can share with others (family, community and/or team):

1. _____

2. _____

3. _____

4. _____

5. _____

What makes these stories so great? Were you an underdog who ended up being triumphant? Was it a special moment with your spouse? Your child? Your family? Your team? Was it the first time you jumped out of an airplane?

1. _____

2. _____

3. _____

4. _____

5. _____

Now identify three "personal worst" stories which you can share with others. What makes these events sad, difficult, unpleasant or frustrating? Was it the death of a family member? The loss of a job? Something you failed to accomplish? How did you overcome these events? How did they make you better, wiser or stronger? How do you handle the pain when you think about these events?

1. _____

   _____

   _____

   _____

2. _____

   _____

   _____

3. _____

   _____

   _____

Correlation

1. At your next opportunity, share a personal best or a personal worst story with your family, community or team and explain how the story relates to the issue at hand.

2. Allow your family members to share a personal best story and a personal worst story. Have them explain how they felt while going through this event as well as what they learned from the experience. What a great family activity at the end of each week!!

3. For the next six team meetings allow one team member to share a personal best story as it relates to the topic at hand. Of course, you, as the extraordinary leader should go first to set the example, tone and pace!

Application

Words of comfort, skillfully administered, are the oldest therapy known to man.
~ Louis Nizer, 1902-1994 ~

Yes, I hear some of my military compatriots shouting about now! Extraordinary leaders also understand that there is a boundary, especially in life, death or combat situations. There are times you must make decisions that are not popular or based on personal feelings you may have for your team members. During Desert Storm, I was a commander of a computer-communications flight. One Saturday morning, I received a message from the communications center requesting names of some of my team members who could be selected to go to the front line. At that point, personal feelings could not be involved in the decision. The decision had to be based on what was best for the mission. Your goal is to be balance the relationship you have with your team members with your responsibility to your company's mission.

Extraordinary leaders can be touched by the hurt of others!

Your Additional Thoughts

_____

_____

_____

_____

_____

_____

_____

_____

_____

_____

_____

_____

_____

_____

_____

Make a Decision!

Continuously Making Effective Decisions is the Norm for

Extraordinary Leaders

1. Observation
2. Interpretation – How Do You Make Decisions?
3. Correlation
4. Application

Observation

Making the right decisions is seldom easy. Situations change and choices confound. Faulty perceptions and biases can block clear thinking and undermine a person's ability to weigh alternatives rationally. As U.S. Supreme Court Justice Benjamin N. Cardozo explained 90 years ago, "We may try to see things as objectively as we please. Nonetheless, we can never see them with any eyes except our own." This is the vexing paradox involved in making decisions: people who are in the process of deciding cannot always trust their own perceptions and thought processes.

Every day we are faced with tens of thousands of choices: from the moment we make the decision to wake up in the morning to the moment we make the decision to go to bed in the evening we are making decisions. Being able to make effective and powerful decisions about every aspect of our lives is the foundation of personal success. In 2005, Peter Drucker wrote that we must learn to manage ourselves, learn to develop others and know how to place ourselves where we can make the greatest contributions. In managing yourself, you must know who you are your strengths and your areas in which you can improve. Your strengths as this is what your foundation is built upon – your areas for improvement are possible cracks in your foundation.

One tool used by Drucker for over 20 years to learn more about himself was through self assessment (his feedback analysis process).

Whenever he made a key decision (or took a key action), he wrote down what he expected to happen. Nine – twelve months later, he compared the actual results with his original expectations. Practiced on a consistent basis, this shows, over a short period of time (2 – 3 years), your strengths in making effective/impactful decisions. This process also outlines what you are doing (or failing to do) which deprives you of the full impact of your strengths.

Have you ever taken the time to think about your decisions … your choices?

Interpretation – How Do You Make Decisions?

Concepts and Definitions

1. Information. This is knowledge about the decision, the effects of its alternatives, the probability of each alternative and so forth. A major point to make here is that while substantial information is desirable, the statement that *the more information, the better* is not true. Too much information can actually reduce the quality of a decision.

2. Alternatives. These are the possibilities one has to choose from. Alternatives can be identified (that is, searched for and located) or even developed (created where they did not previously exist). Merely searching for preexisting alternatives will often result in less effective decision making.

3. Criteria. These are the characteristics or requirements that each alternative must possess to a greater or lesser extent. Usually the alternatives are rated on how well they possess each criterion.

4. Goals. What is it you want to accomplish? Strangely enough, many decision makers collect a bunch of alternatives (say potential trips to take or prospective people to marry) and then ask, "Which should I choose?" without thinking first of what their goals are and what overall objective they want to achieve. Next time you find yourself asking, "What should I do? What should I choose?", first ask yourself "What are my goals?" A component of goal identification should be included in every instance of decision analysis.

5. Value. Value refers to how desirable a particular outcome is. The value of the alternatives can be measured in dollars, satisfaction or another benefit.

6. Preferences. These reflect the philosophy and moral hierarchy of the decision maker. We could say that they are the decision maker's "values," but that might be confusing with the other use of the word, above. If we could use that word here, we would say that personal values dictate preferences. Some people prefer excitement to calmness, certainty to risk, efficiency to esthetics, quality to quantity, and so on. Thus, when one person chooses to ride the wildest roller coaster in the park and another chooses a mild ride, both may be making good decisions based on their individual preferences.

7. Decision Quality. This is a rating of whether a decision is good or bad. A good decision is a logical one based on the available information and reflecting the preferences of the decision maker.

The important concept to grasp here is that the quality of a decision is not related to its outcome: a good decision can have either a good or a bad outcome. Similarly, a bad decision, one not based on adequate information or not reflecting the decision maker's preferences, can still have a good outcome.

Some Decision Making Strategies

As you know, there are often many solutions to a given problem, and the decision maker's task is to choose one of them. The task of choosing can be as simple or as complex as the importance of the decision warrants, and the number and quality of alternatives can also be adjusted according to importance, time, resources and so on. There are several strategies used for choosing. Robert Harris (http://wwww.virtualsalt.com/crebok6a.htm, 2009) shares the following:

1. Optimizing. This is the strategy of choosing the best possible solution to the problem, discovering as many alternatives as possible and choosing the very best. How thoroughly optimizing can be done is dependent on:

> A. importance of the problem
> B. time available for solving it
> C. cost involved with alternative solutions
> D. availability of resources, knowledge
> E. personal psychology, values

Note that the collection of complete information and the consideration of all alternatives is seldom possible for most major decisions, so limitations must be placed on alternatives.

2. Satisficing. In this strategy, the first satisfactory alternative is chosen rather than the best alternative. If you are very hungry, you might choose to stop at the first decent looking restaurant in the next town rather than attempting to choose the best restaurant from among all (the optimizing strategy). The word *satisficing* was coined by combining *satisfactory* and *sufficient*. For many small decisions, such as where to park, what to drink, which pen to use, which tie to wear, and so on, the satisficing strategy is perfect.

3. Maximax. This stands for "maximize the maximums." This strategy focuses on evaluating and then choosing the alternatives based on their maximum possible payoff. This is sometimes described as the strategy of the optimist, because favorable outcomes and high potentials are the areas of concern. It is a good strategy for use when risk taking is most acceptable, when the go-for-broke philosophy is reigning freely.

4. Maximin. This stands for "maximize the minimums." In this strategy, that of the pessimist, the worst possible outcome of each decision is considered and the decision with the highest minimum is chosen. The Maximin orientation is good when the consequences of a failed decision are particularly harmful or undesirable. Maximin concentrates on the salvage value of a decision, or of the guaranteed return of the decision. It's the philosophy behind the saying, "A bird in the hand is worth two in the bush."

Quiz shows exploit the uncertainty many people feel when they are not quite sure whether to go with a maximax strategy or a maximin one: "Okay, Mrs. Freen, you can now choose to take what you've already won and go home, or risk losing it all and find out what's behind door number three."

Decision Making Procedure

In a typical decision making situation, as you move from step to step here, you will probably find yourself moving back and forth also.

1. Identify the decision to be made along with the goals it should achieve. Determine the scope and limitations of the decision. Is the new job to be permanent or temporary or is that not yet known (thus requiring another decision later)? Is the new package for the product to be put into all markets or just into a test market? How might the scope of the decision be changed; that is, what are its possible parameters?

When thinking about the decision, be sure to include a clarification of goals. We must decide whom to hire for our new secretary, *one who will be able to create an efficient and organized office.* Or, we must decide where to go on vacation, *where we can relax and get some rest from the fast pace of society.*

2. Get the facts. But remember that you cannot get all the facts. Get as many facts as possible about a decision within the limits of time imposed on you and your ability to process them, but remember that virtually every decision must be made in partial ignorance. Lack of complete information must not be allowed to paralyze your decision. A decision based on partial knowledge is usually better than not making the decision when a decision is really needed. The proverb that "any decision is better than no decision," while perhaps extreme, shows the importance of choosing. When you are racing toward a bridge support, you must decide to turn away to the right or to the left. Which way you turn is less important than the fact that you do indeed turn.

As part of your collection of facts, list your feelings, hunches, and intuitive urges. Many decisions must ultimately rely on or be influenced by intuition because of the remaining degree of uncertainty involved in the situation.

As part of your collection of facts, consult those who will be affected by the decision and those who will have to implement it. Input from these people not only helps supply you with information and assistance in making the decision, but it helps the implementers feel that they are part of the decision-making process, making them more accepting of the decision and the changes it will bring about. As Russell Ackoff noted in *The Art of Problem Solving*, not consulting people involved in a decision is often perceived as an act of aggression.

3. Develop alternatives. Make a list of all the possible choices you have, including the choice of doing nothing. Not choosing one of the candidates or one of the building sites is in itself a decision. Often, a non-decision is harmful, as mentioned above, not choosing to turn either right or left is to choose to drive into the bridge. But sometimes the decision to do nothing is useful or at least better than the alternatives, so it should always be consciously included in the decision-making process.

Be sure to think about not just identifying available alternatives, but creating alternatives that don't yet exist. *For example, if you want to choose which major to pursue in college, think not only of the ones available in the catalog, but of designing your own course of study.*

4. Rate each alternative. This is the evaluation of the value of each alternative. Consider the negative of each alternative (cost, consequences, problems created, time needed, etc.) and the positive of each (money saved, time saved, added creativity or happiness to company or employees, etc.). Remember here that the alternative that you might like best or that would in the best of all possible worlds be an obvious choice may not be functional in the real world because of too much cost, time, or lack of acceptance by others.

Don't forget to include indirect factors in the rating. If you are deciding between machines X, Y, and Z and you already have an employee who knows how to operate machine Z, that fact should be considered. If you are choosing an investigative team to send to Japan to look at plant sites and you have very qualified candidates A, B, and C, the fact that B is a very fast typist, a superior photographer or has some other side benefit in addition to being a qualified team member, should be considered. In fact, what you put on the hobbies and interests line of your resume can be quite important when you apply for a job simply because employers are interested in getting people with a good collection of additional abilities.

5. Rate the risk of each alternative. In problem solving, you hunt around for a solution that best solves a particular problem, and by the end of such a hunt you are pretty sure that the solution will work. In decision making, however, there is always some degree of uncertainty in any choice. Will Bill really work out as the new supervisor? If we decide to expand into Canada, will our sales and profits really increase? If we let Jane date Fred at age fifteen, will the experience be good? If you decide to marry person X or buy car Y or go to school Z, will that be the best choice or at least a satisfactory choice?

Risks can be rated as percentages, ratios, rankings, grades or in any other form that allows them to be compared. See the section on risk evaluation for more details on risking.

6. Make the decision. If you are making an individual decision, apply your preferences (which may take into account the preferences of others). Choose the path to follow, whether it includes one of the alternatives, more than one of them (a multiple decision) or the decision to choose none.

After you've made your decision, don't forget to implement the it and then evaluate the implementation, just as you would in a problem solving experience.

One important item often overlooked in implementation is that when explaining the decision to those involved in carrying it out or those who will be affected by it, you shouldn't list only the projected benefits; instead, frankly explain the risks and drawbacks involved and tell why you believe the proposed benefits outweigh the negatives. Implementers are much more willing to support decisions when they (1) understand the risks and (2) believe that they are being treated with honesty and like adults.

Remember also that very few decisions are irrevocable. Don't cancel a decision prematurely because many new plans require time to work - it may take years for your new branch office in Paris to become profitable - but don't hesitate to change directions if a particular decision clearly is not working out or is being somehow harmful. You can always make another decision to do something else

Correlation

For the next 12 months, like Drucker, begin to journal your decisions using the following outline:

Issue to be resolved or decided upon: _____
_____
_____
_____
_____

Desired outcome: _____
_____
_____
_____
_____

Alternative decisions to consider and select from: _____
_____
_____
_____
_____

Decision selected: _____
_____
_____
_____
_____

Expected outcome: _____
_____
_____
_____
_____

Actual outcome: _____
_____
_____
_____
_____

Alignment to expected outcome and desired results? _____
_____
_____
_____
_____

Application

As decision makers, we are prone to be overconfident in our occasional success and over generalize the degree to which good intuitive solutions to some dynamic problem also offer good solutions to other problems.

~Robert J. Meyer & Wesley Hutchinson ~

Each day we are faced with so many situations which require a decision; many times we make a decision without even thinking about it. For example, which route should you take to get home tonight?

Other times, the decision required is so taxing, so weighty that we put off making the decision as long as possible. In both cases, very seldom do we take the time to review our decisions (or our personal decision making process) for its effectiveness, its impact, its repeatability or its alignment with our own value system (or the value system of the organization we represent).

During the latter portion of the 20th Century, many decisions had to be made which cost others their very livelihood (financial crises, housing crises, etc.). How would it have been different if the decision makers had selected a value based effective decision making process?

Extraordinary Leaders make effective, repeatable, values based decisions!

Your Additional Thoughts

_____

_____

_____

_____

_____

_____

_____

_____

_____

_____

_____

_____

_____

_____

Visionary
Extraordinary Leaders Set the Vision

1. Observation
2. Interpretation - What Is Your Vision?
3. Correlation
4. Application

Observation

Every great idea, every movement starts with the vision of one person. This person does not see all the steps required to obtain the vision; however, he or she does have a picture of what the vision will do once it is implemented.

Extraordinary Leaders understand they must surround themselves with great people and great teams to accomplish the vision. Your vision will require resources to implement. Because you are on purpose, the resources you require are surrounding you – ready to move forward. In other words, another person's purpose is to assist you in achieving your vision and your purpose is to be in place to assist someone in achieving their vision.

Expect and look for existing resources (individuals, teams, partners, vendors, other departments) to assist you in achieving your vision. Do not be so proud that you cannot accept the help of others. Stop yourself from overlooking what is right in front of you just because it looks old or damaged.

Vision allows you to do great things with old stuff!

Relax. Close your eyes. Inhale deeply. Exhale all the air out of your body. Do this about 10 times. Now, begin to think about your life. What is it you see yourself doing to make the world better, to make your family better, to make the lives of your family better?

What is it that you see? Stay in that moment. What does it feel like to be in that space? Inhale again. Now what does it really feel like to be in that space? Who is there with you? How do they feel? Inhale the vision; exhale the thoughts associated with that vision. Imagine … Imagine … Imagine. Now, for each area in your life, complete the following exercise:

What Is Your Vision?

The vision I have for my life is: _____

_____
_____
_____
_____
_____
_____
_____

The organization I belong to has the following vision: _____

_____
_____
_____
_____
_____

Our team (family or organization) vision is: _____

_____
_____
_____
_____
_____
_____
_____
_____

Correlation

1. Identify 5 resources you need to accomplish your personal vision:

   a. _____

   _____

   _____

   b. _____

   _____

   _____

   c. _____

   _____

   _____

   d. _____

   _____

   _____

   e. _____

   _____

   _____

2. Who provides the resources you identified above?

   a. _____

   _____

   _____

   b. _____

   _____

   _____

c._____

_____

_____

d._____

_____

_____

e._____

_____

_____

3. In order to accomplish our team's vision, we need the following five resources:

a._____

_____

_____

b._____

_____

_____

c._____

_____

_____

d._____

_____

_____

e. _____

_____

_____

4. Who can provide the resources we need as a team?

   a._____
   _____

   b._____
   _____

   c._____
   _____

   d._____
   _____

   e._____
   _____

5. Who on our team will be responsible for working with the resources required to achieve our vision?

   a._____
   _____

   b._____
   _____

   c._____
   _____

   d._____
   _____

   e. _____
   _____

6. As a team, whose vision are we responsible for realizing?

    a._____

    _____

    b._____

    _____

    c._____

    _____

7. Who within our team will reach out to those identified Question (#6)?

    a._____

    _____

    b._____

    _____

    c. _____

    _____

8. Build a vision board with pictures and words linked to your accomplished vision (even though it has not been accomplished). Build the board with pictures of what your vision will look like once you've accomplished it. Take 15 minutes each day to look at your vision board. In your mind, experience what each area will feel like, smell like, taste like, etc.

    During this time, live in your vision. For example, on my vision board I have pictures of two villas in Jamaica which I will own – so for 15 minutes each day, I imagine what it feels like to sit on the patio, looking over the golf course and fixing my gaze on the ocean, feeling the ocean breeze across my face, seeing my family enjoying themselves, eating all the wonderful food prepared by our chef.

By doing this you are giving your mind an imprint – it becomes reality to your mind. Find the words to support this vision. Don't worry about the how-tos at this point, just think about being already there. Then watch the doors being opened, the connections being made. Once the vision is rooted in your heart and your words align with that vision – the resources will appear.

9. Begin to write in your journal what this experience will be like. Who is there with you? What are you doing? What does it feel like? Enjoy the 15 minutes.

Application

There is nothing like a dream to create the future.
~ Victor Hugo, 1802-1885 ~

I hear your screams about now... "Dr. Stephanie is just asking for too much! Now I've got to close my eyes!" We're all familiar with "the rat race". My vision of this race is being on a hamster wheel running at full speed, going no-where. Why does the conception of "the rat race" conjure up this image? Could it be that it's because we don't take the time to figure out the best path to get out of the race? What if you spent 15 minutes just thinking about the end state of a vision as opposed to all that is required to get there? It is the vision that keeps you moving forward. How cool would it be for this to be a family or team event? Once a week, consider gathering as a family or team to consider an issue which must be solved. Ask the participants to envision the end state. If you encourage a free format or free forming discussion, you will receive the most amazing results!

For many years, I've used my refrigerator as a place to display my vision. It is one place I know I'll visit at least three times a day. This year, I've moved my vision to the closet doors in my home office. Covering every aspect of my life - spiritual, mental, relational, financial and physical - I have a visual for the desired end state. When I'm stuck, I take five minutes to look at the board. When I've had a frustrating day, I take five minutes to look at the board. When I've had a victory, I look at the board. These impromptu visits to my vision board, in addition to the fifteen minutes I spend each week thinking about my overall vision, provides me with a sense of peace, purpose and accomplishment. Do me a favor … just do it!

Every great idea and every great movement starts with the vision of one person. This extraordinary leader may not see all the pieces; however, they do see the final state, the final picture.

Extraordinary leaders understand that the vision will require resources and are humble enough to accept these resources when they are presented by others.

Extraordinary leaders have vision!

Your Additional Thoughts

_____

_____

_____

_____

_____

_____

_____

_____

_____

_____

_____

_____

_____

_____

Sponsorship
Extraordinary Leaders Ensure They Are Being Groomed & Are Grooming Others

1. Observation
2. Interpretation -- What Slice of PIE Are You Working On Today?
3. Correlation
4. Application

Observation

- Sponsorship is very different from mentorship
  - Being mentored
    - allows an individual to train, educate, lead and guide; however, their scope of authority may not extend to the levels in which you need to succeed
    - allows you to select your mentor
    - is VERY important, you will want to have multiple mentors within your organization as well as outside of your organization

  - Being sponsored means
    - being hand-selected by someone one or more levels above you (within your organization or your community)
    - being groomed by someone who lets the world know that he or she is grooming you
    - being advocated for by someone who will pick up the phone to call others and direct them (highly encourage them) to select you for a position within their company (even if your sponsor does not belong to that company)

- being selected to lead key projects (ahead of others who have been with the company longer, who are qualified, and who are more experienced)
- your opportunities for failing forward are much higher than just failing
- being favored (YES, favoritism still exists - and that is GOOD!)

- Your selection for promotion is related to a success formula created by Harvey Coleman in his book *Empowering Yourself* (1996). It is a very simple formula -- P.I.E.
  - **P**erformance - How well are you able to perform the tasks which have been assigned to you?
  - **I**mage - Do you fit the corporate image? Do you fit the executive level corporate image?
  - **E**xposure - To whom do you have access and what level are they at within the organization?

- **PERFORMANCE**
  - You are expected to perform at the level into which you have been hired; however, are you performing at higher levels?
  - The higher you go within an organization, the less this becomes an issue. For example, when you first entered your career field, you were expected to be a specialist; as you are promoted to the higher levels you must know enough about the areas for which you are responsible. At this point you become more of a generalist.
  - You are expected to stay abreast of trends, changes and technology as it impacts your discipline. TIP FOR SUCCESS: Use your learning teams!

- **IMAGE**

  - When leaders within your organization speak of you what words do they use to describe you – Leader, Can-

Do-It Person, Our Next Vice President, Always Late, Not a Team Player, Dishonest, Always Angry?

- Labels, whether or not they are based on truth, have a tendency to stick. Your job is to find out which labels have been assigned to you and if necessary begin a campaign to change the label to something more positive.

o What do the leaders at the executive level look like?
  - Business Suits (Tailored or Off the Rack)
  - Business Casual
  - Casual
  - Remember to dress at the level you desire to be, not at your current level

o Take the extra steps to identify what image you are presenting and work with the appropriate experts to make improvements. Consider meeting with an executive coach, a professional coach, an image consultant, a communications consultant or another professional who can help you improve your image.

- **EXPOSURE**

  o Exposure is your access to leaders within your organization and within your community.

  o How often are you asked to present to senior leadership? If not once a quarter or more often, volunteer to present to leadership. Join key focus groups which can provide you exposure to leaders outside of your organization.

  o Look for opportunities to represent your organization on non-profit boards or key campaigns.

        o   Look for opportunities to speak to organizations outside of your own organization.

What slice of PIE are you working on today?

At the beginning of your career, your concentration must be on your **performance**. You must stand out as the person the organization can ALWAYS count on to:

- Get the Job Done
- Solve Complex Problems
- Know Industry Trends
- Possess the Ability to Train Others
- Act as the "Go To" Person

Once you've identified yourself as the one who can get the job done; begin to work on your **image**. Find out what your organization thinks about you as a total person.

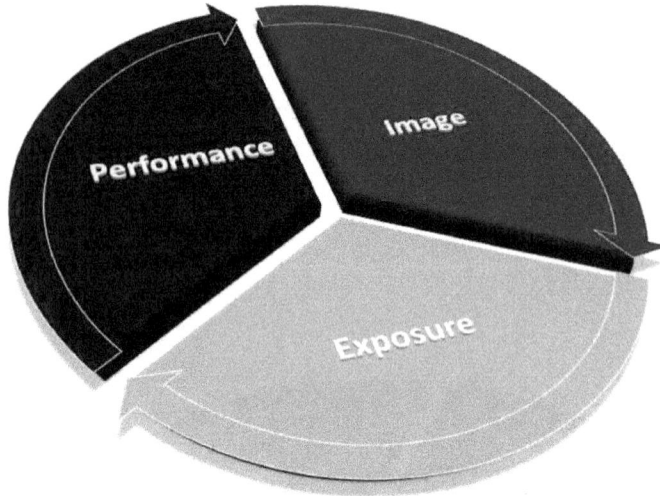

- **At this time you <u>MUST</u> ask yourself, *"Do I want to do what it takes to 'fit in' at that level?"***
- Do they see you as fitting their corporate image?
- Do they see you as READY for promotion?
- Look up 2 - 3 levels would you fit into the group at that level?
- Does your attire match theirs?
  - Do they always wear suits?
  - Are their shoes always polished?
- Are you playing where they play?
  - Golf?
  - Tennis?
  - Spades?
  - Dominos?
  - Cash Flow?
- Do they make a point of
  - Going to lunch with each other
  - Going shopping together
  - Going on vacation together
  - Spending their weekends together

Two quick tips: Find an executive coach certified to deliver leadership assessments and a certified image consultant. Have them walk through the building with you and then spend the time, energy, effort and money to use their services for at least three to nine months.

Contact our office for references on these tips!!!

Have you ever wondered why some people are afforded opportunities when there are more qualified people? Many of us know of better singers, better speakers, better writers, better programmers, better leaders or better _____ than those who are making the headlines today. What separated them from the rest of the pack? It was the **exposure** they were provided by their sponsor. They were selected to lead a key project and with the help of their sponsor and their team, they succeeded. They had their first opportunity at being **exposed** to the organization and/or to the world.

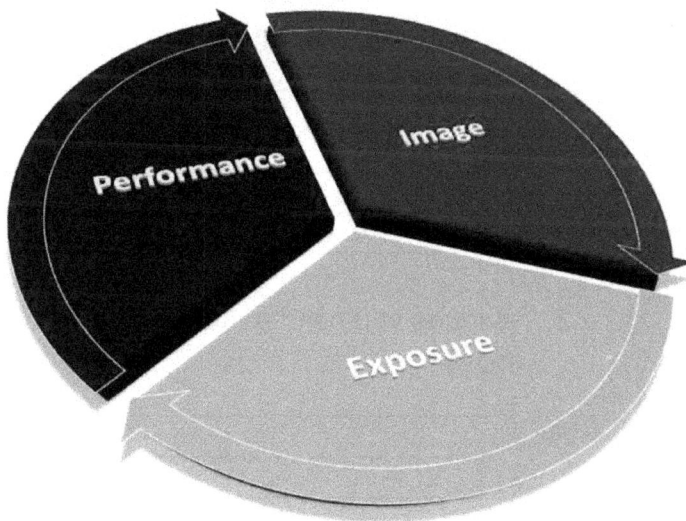

Once your name is out there others will seek you out for key opportunities. They will seek you based on a recommendation from your sponsor and based on seeing you representing the organization at various events. (This is why your image must match the organization's image - the corporate image!). This is why so many people are "looking for that one big break"; once it breaks, the only element which can stop you is the person you're looking at in the mirror.

Correlation

1. Draw two circles:
   1. The first circle represents today. Draw your own PIE. Where are you today? Is your performance piece completely full? Is it solid? If you asked your leader, would he or she draw the same picture?
   2. The next circle represents the next 120 days. Draw the PIE you would like to see develop. Complete this exercise at least twice a year.

      1. What do you need to do in order to see a change in your Performance?
         a. _____
         b. _____
         c. _____
         d. _____
         e. _____

      2. What do you need to do to see a change in your Image?
         a. _____
         b. _____
         c. _____
         d. _____
         e. _____

    3. What do you need to do to see your PIE change as it relates to your Exposure?

       a. _____

       b. _____

       c. _____

       d. _____

       e. _____

2. Ask the people within your Holy of Holies to complete the same exercise about you. Where do they see you? After they have done this, show them your desired state and ask them to make recommendations on what you need to do to get to your desired state. Ask them to hold you accountable for this action plan.

3. Identify

    1. A key company project that you can become part of or lead: _____

       1. Meet with the executive owner and obtain their permission to join the team.

       2. Meet with your leader and obtain their permission to join the team.

    2. A key non-profit organization your company supports: _____

       1. Meet with your Community Relations Department Executive and find out what you need to do to represent your organization on this board.

       2. Obtain permission from your leader to sit on this board.

4. If your organization has an executive coaching program or a mentoring program ask your leader for permission to participate in the program. Do this within the next 15 days.

Application

The greatest good you can do for another is not just to share your riches, but to reveal to him his own.
~ Benjamin Disraeli, 1804-1881 ~

Sponsorship is perhaps the one leadership characteristic which is feared by some leaders, thought to be unfair by many and accepted as the status quo by others. The topic of the "Good 'Ole Boy Network" recently became a highlight of a discussion with a bank vice president. The VP thought that this system was unfair and should be removed from the workplace. I shared with her and others that this network is simply a form of sponsorship. In most cases a person is not promoted unless they can do the job (performance).

However, how quickly a person rises through the ranks is really based on how well they fit into the company success profile (image) and how much they are seen (exposure).

Out of the three (performance, image and exposure), image usually causes more concerns. Image means you do what is necessary to fit into the corporate picture. It's a choice. For some, it may mean assimilating or conforming. For example, let's say that on the weekends you really enjoy just hanging out with your friends; however you've noticed that Bob makes it a point to get up every other Saturday to play golf at the same golf course where his CEO plays. Bob made a choice to ensure his image matches that of his CEO AND that he has exposure to his CEO outside of the office. Do you have to take such actions? ABSOLUTELY NOT! It is, however, a choice you must make, a choice which can have a major impact on how fast you move up in the workplace and how far you go.

I'll share a personal example. While working at a former company, I asked the head of HR (SVP) what I needed to do to get promoted within the company. Her response – "Exposure. You should represent the company by sitting on a board or two." My response – Within 90 days, I became a board member with three different organizations supported by my company. Side note: During an offsite meeting with my boss and peers, they shared that they thought it was unfair that I sat on boards and that our boss should have found positions for them to take on as well. Hmmm? Did they not understand that they are responsible for their own careers?

Final comment – If you've made it to the top, you have no reason to be afraid to sponsor others to success.

Performance is expected
Image is watched to determine how well you fit into the group
Exposure is provided to few.

Your Additional Thoughts

_____

_____

_____

_____

_____

_____

_____

_____

_____

_____

_____

_____

_____

_____

Legacy

What are you leaving ahead?

1. Observation
2. Interpretation - Who has your thumbprint on their future?
3. Correlation
4. Application

Observation

The best gift an extraordinary leader can give is a better future. That is why I want you to think about leaving a legacy ahead and not behind. Think generationally when you think of legacy! Many believe that they have to change the world to make a difference. However, I believe that if you can make one person's life better, you can change the world. For example, if you teach a child to read and that child grows up to be the doctor who creates a cure for cancer, what legacy have you left ahead (yes ahead)! One small deed will change the world.

You have the opportunity to leave a legacy ahead through mentoring and/or sponsoring someone. Mentoring is providing guidance and direction and an ear when necessary. Sponsoring is making something happen for someone else that will position them to go to a higher level.

When you mentor people, you meet with them on a periodic basis to help them grow in the various aspects of their lives. Protégés may ask you to assist them in developing their financial skills, presentation skills or even parenting skills. You, then, based on your own expertise assist them in areas in which they need to grow. You might provide them with a list of activities to complete, a series of books to read or even set aside a time during which you will meet with them to help them improve their proficiency in a particular area. Extraordinary leaders know that they should have more than one mentor.

Finding mentors in every area of your life is the rule not the exception.

To understand what sponsorship is, allow me to tell a true story (with names changed to protect all). John, a thirty-five year old low level manager (compensation ~$35K/year) discovered that his college did not have a statue to honor his university's founder. So he formed a committee to plan for the creation and placement of such a statue.

John found the best people to sit on the board of this specific committee. He presented the idea to a specific philanthropist who agreed to sit on this board. Over time the philanthropist became so impressed with John that he hired him. The philanthropist provided him with a position which required all agencies requesting funds (or partnerships) to go through John.

He set up John's office outside of his office (on the right side). The philanthropist multiplied John's salary by five. The philanthropist then introduced John to the world as his "go-to" guy. He then introduced John to his lawyers, his builder and others who could assist in bringing John up to a higher level.

Do you see the difference between being mentored and being sponsored?

Who are you mentoring? Who are you sponsoring? Who is mentoring you? Who is sponsoring you?

Who has your thumbprint on their future?

a. Identify four people who you currently mentor. Why are you mentoring them? How are you measuring their success?

_____

_____

_____

_____

b. Identify one person you are sponsoring. Why did you select this person to sponsor? How are you ensuring their success?

_____

_____

_____

_____

Correlation

a. Identify two additional people you can mentor in your community.

_____

_____

b. Why did you select these two people?

Person 1: _____

_____

_____

Person 2: _____

_____

_____

c. What are your 30-, 60-, 90- day objectives for these two individuals?

Person 1: _____

_____

_____

_____

Person 2: _____

_____

_____

_____

d. Select a person who you can sponsor to success.

_____

e. Why did you select this person? _____

_____

_____

f. What will you do to ensure their success? _____

_____

_____

_____

_____

_____

Application

The legacy of heroes is the memory of a great name and the
inheritance of a great example.
~ Benjamin Disraeli, 1804-1881~

My firm belief is that our biggest impact can be made by doing the little things. One person I know continues to build her legacy by simply opening her high profile network to young men and women from impoverished communities. Last year, I received an email from one of my previous administrative assistants - I had not heard from her in over ten years. She shared that she was a now a vice president and would not have even considered going after such an opportunity if I had not challenged her to think about her future and envision what she wanted to do the rest of her life. Your thumbprint on a person's life can cause that person to discover a cure for cancer. Your thumbprint on a person's life can give them enough hope to continue living. Your thumbprint will birth greatness!

Who is standing on your shoulders?

Extraordinary leaders take the time to make a difference in the lives of others – with no applause expected!

Your Additional Thoughts

_____

_____

_____

_____

_____

_____

_____

_____

_____

_____

_____

_____

_____

Final Thoughts

The time is always right to do what is right.
– Martin Luther King, Jr., 1929-1968 –

We started this manual by congratulating you for beginning your leadership journey. I firmly believe that if you really take this manual to heart and practice all the activities you learn on a daily basis that you will see a difference in your leadership ability.

Remember, this leadership manual is built on the foundation of the premise that leadership is a privilege, an honor and a choice you must make every day.

Keeping the mindset that you must know how to lead yourself before leading teams and lead teams before you are given the responsibility of leading organizations. Keeping this strategy in mind at all times allows you to become more effective in the 21st century.

A word of caution – this is a continuous learning process. In other words, you will repeat each step over and over and over again in your leadership journey. In fact, you will want to pull this manual out each time you make any type of change in any aspect of your life and/or when you find yourself slipping into previous behaviors.

Your mastery and expertise in leadership is dependent upon you repeating the steps in this book often.

Remember, however, you are not alone! There are thousands who are reading this book at the same time and are currently sharing ideas in a "member's only" The New Face of Leadership LinkedIn group – which I encourage you to join!

Also, feel free to reach out to me at DrStephanieParson@CrownedGrace.com with any questions! Finally, thank you for adding The Character of a Leader to your leadership journey.

Your Final Thoughts

_____

_____

_____

_____

_____

_____

_____

_____

_____

_____

_____

_____

_____

_____

_____

_____

_____

_____

_____

_____

_____

_____

_____

_____

_____

_____

_____

_____

_____

_____

_____

_____

_____

_____

_____

_____

_____

_____

_____

_____

_____

_____

_____

_____

Stephanie A. Parson, Ph.D.

"Are you living an extraordinary life – today?"

Stephanie A. Parson – President Ph.D., MA, BS

Dr Parson is a proven consultant, speaker, author and executive with global Fortune 500 experience in leading teams in the public and private sectors. She possesses over 20 years of charismatic leadership, executive management and extensive problem solving skills in strategic planning, talent development and organizational change. Dr. Parson has conducted leadership development events for more than 6000 individuals within the public and private sector in the United States, Mexico and Brazil.

Dr. Parson's background includes roles in executive management, strategic planning and program management. As an executive coach, she has provided guidance to many leaders within the private and public sectors. Prior to creating Crowned Grace she served as a Vice President at Walt Disney World, where her duties entailed day-to-day operations of the strategic planning process, research and development, the fiscal planning process, procurement, the Program Management Office, Training and productivity improvement. She implemented the first strategic planning process for Walt Disney World's IT Group, leading to a Strategic Plan (Balanced Scorecard). She also implemented the first Program Management Office for Walt Disney World, leading to a rollout of standard practices for project management across the Walt Disney Company. In this role, her team sourced and delivered more than 1200 training seats and implemented a training provider network.

Dr Parson's other leadership experience includes serving as the Vice President and Chief Information Officer for Parsons Brinckerhoff Inc., one of the world's oldest continuously operating engineering firms. Ranked number one in transportation engineering, the firm has major practice areas in energy, power, aviation planning and environmental and facilities in over 200 offices worldwide with more than 8000 employees. Dr. Parson also led a global staff of 112 professionals for new development and ongoing support for Seagram Spirits and Wine Group. As a Director, she owned financial responsibility for a $15M annual operating budget with a separate $24M capital budget. Additionally, Dr Parson is a decorated military veteran, having served as an officer in the United States Air Force prior to entering the corporate sector.

She holds a BS in Computer Science, Dual MA in Management and Computer Resources Management, Masters Certificate in Project Management, Masters Certificate in Business Administration, a PhD in Philosophy and is currently working on her doctorate in business administration. Dr. Parson is certified in Total Quality Management and certified to deliver various leadership assessments.

Dr. Parson's articles and comments on leadership and technology can be found on-line as well as in print in various newspapers and magazines.

Other Products & Services

1. Consulting Services
2. Leadership Development & Professional Development Workshops
3. Additional Products
4. Contact Us

People Transformation

* Leadership Development   * Employee Development   * Executive Coaching   *

The organization's performance is powered by the effective use of financial capital, technological capital and human capital. In a world in which businesses must compete in an ever widening arena while doing more with less, human capital has emerged as elusive to quantify and the most critical to business success. CGI specializes in the people part of a successful business strategy, helping you manage people issues and opportunities enabling your organization to perform to its full potential!

Technology Transformation

* Applications Portfolio   * Knowledge Management   * IT Governance   * Risk & Compliance *

The global IT landscape is changing rapidly. The fast moving market trends and evolution of new technologies are crafting the future model of the next generation business environment. Organizations are under immense pressure to adopt to these new trends and adopt new and emerging technologies to keep pace with competitors. At CGI, we provide future enabled technology-driven solutions to our customers which transform the existing IT platforms within the organization.

Business Transformation

* Strategic Planning * Supply Chain Management * Change
Management * Process Reengineering *

The competitive environment with increasing customer demand for innovation and higher value is transforming the current business processes in all industries. Business leaders are looking for new business models which are aligned to changed business scenarios to improve productivity, efficiency, market share and profitability in the market place. At CGI, we understand the changing trends and offer services to clients to satisfy the demands for innovation and higher value from their customers. We expedite the implementation and application of new business models.

Workshops Include:

Leading Yourself
- Maximizing Your Personal Effectiveness (LS501)
- Emotionally Intelligent Management & Leadership Strategies (LS502)
- Communication, Negotiation & Presentation Skills (LS503)
- Innovative Leadership Competencies (LS506)
- Values & Ethics – Foundational To Your Success (LS506)
- Time Management (LS507)

Leading Teams
- Leadership & Management Skills for Supervisors (LT602)
- Leadership & Team Development for Managerial Success (LT603)
- Managing Conflict, Change & Handling Difficult People (LT604)
- Motivating, Managing & Leading Teams (LT605)
- Leadership & Management Skills for the 21st Century (LT606)
- The Art of Leadership (LT607)
- Creative Vision, Goal Setting & Strategy (LT609)
- Effective Decision Making for Maximum Impact (LT610)
- The Power of Diversity (LT611)

Leading Organizations
- Leadership, Vision & Organizational Reality (LO701)
- Advanced Leadership Skills (LO702)
- Motivation, Strategic Planning & Creative Problem Solving (LO703)
- Advanced Leadership & Management Skills (LO704)
- Practical Strategies for Organizational Success (LO705)
- Improving Performance Through the Balanced Scorecard (LO706)
- Building a Climate for Innovation Through Transformational Leadership (LO707)

Additional Programs Designed For Your Success
- The Project Professional (LA801)
- Project Planning, Scheduling & Control (LA802)
- IT Project Management (LA803)
- Developing Internal Customer Services (LA804)
- Customer Service (LA805)

Certified To Deliver the Following Leadership Assessments
- The Hogan Leadership Forecast Series
- DiSC®
- MBTI®
- Emotional Quotient Inventory (EQi)
- Thomas-Kilmann Conflict Mode Instrument (TKI)
- Discovering Diversity Profile
- FIRO-B®
- Many other industry standard assessments

4. Contact Us: 321.251.5236 (o) | 321.251.5242 (f) | 866.544.6257 (Toll Free)

Dr. Parson has captured the true essence of leadership; it is what is at an individual's core that allows them the privilege to lead others. This book encourages you to take inventory and find the balance of mind, body and spirit to be the best possible leader you can be. It is well worth your time to do so and discover your full potential as a leader.
-- Michael Robinson, General Manager, Microsoft - Middle East

"Leaders are not common. This manual is atypical and Dr. Stephanie Parson is certainly uncommon. Her gift and genius has been revealed in this work because she has found the secret; God wants His people to be extraordinary. When we wake up to this revelation, His Spirit makes us unique in purpose, personality, power and performance...key components of leadership. There is then no room for the common or ordinary. She has learned to cultivate and apply a *leadership spirit* which all effective leaders must exemplify and continue to develop...it defines them and enables them to fulfill their purpose. Dr. Parson has accomplished something very few leadership resources have done; she has challenged the mental attitude and aptitude of leaders by requiring them to do something...application. This is truly a self-discovery journey of one's *leadership spirit*...that makes it and you the reader, extraordinary!"
-- John Barker, Co-Founder & SVP, Ark Leisure Group, Inc.

"Dr Parson has synthesized the core truths of what makes great leaders great, and created one of the most useful documents I've ever read on how each of us can make the journey. This is not a "quick read-quick fix", but a great tool to guide you in doing the hard work and introspection necessary to make positive changes. This is the kind of guidance I often wished for as a young officer—and the kind of tool I'm glad to have now that I know what kind of leader I want to become."
-- Ann K. Lee, Lt Colonel, USAF, Retired

"Dr. Stephanie Parson's new book on leadership will prove to be a valuable addition to this important field. Read, reflect and then apply."
-- Pat Williams, Orlando Magic Senior Vice President & Author of *the Pursuit*

Management/Leadership
$27.97
ISBN 978-0-578-04870-3

www.ingramcontent.com/pod-product-compliance
Lightning Source LLC
Chambersburg PA
CBHW080557220326
41599CB00032B/6512